WITHDRAWN

Also by LANZA DEL VASTO

Return to the Source (1972)

*Principles and Precepts
of the Return to the Obvious* (1974)

*From Gandhi to Vinoba:
The New Pilgrimage* (1974)

Make Straight the Way of the Lord (1974)

WARRIORS
OF
PEACE

WARRIORS
OF
PEACE

*Writings on the Technique
of Nonviolence by*

Lanza del Vasto

*Edited by Michel Random
and Translated from the French by
Jean Sidgwick*

ALFRED A. KNOPF • NEW YORK • 1974

THIS IS A BORZOI BOOK
PUBLISHED BY ALFRED A. KNOPF, INC.

Library of Congress Cataloging in Publication Data

Lanza del Vasto, Joseph Jean (Date)   Warriors of peace.

Translation of Technique de la non-violence.
1. Nonviolence.   2. Passive resistance.
3. War and religion.   I. Title.
HM278.L3513   1974   301.6'32   74–2121
ISBN 0–394–48927–6   ISBN 0–394–70933–0 (Pbk)

Manufactured in the United States of America

FIRST EDITION

CONTENTS

Contents

PUBLISHER'S NOTE

Today Lanza del Vasto is the acknowledged leader of the non-violent movement in France. But the seed was sown in 1936, when he left Europe for India in search of true spiritual values. It was there that he met Gandhi, who bestowed on him the name Shantidas (Servant of Peace). Although Lanza would have preferred to remain at Gandhi's feet, he realized that he must return to France and do there what Gandhi had done in India—train a small band of followers to make a stand for justice and for truth. He tells of this pilgrimage in his book *Return to the Source.*

Toward the end of the Second World War Lanza formed a select group that worked together in Paris, and in 1948 the first rural community, the Community of the Ark, was set up at the estate at Tournier. The Ark is a nonsectarian order, open to people of all religions providing they adhere strictly to the tenets of their faith; it is a working order of men and women who put Gandhi's principles into practice in their daily life. The note that is sounded constantly is this: "The aim of manual labor is not only to obtain one's daily bread by pure means, but to bring about an inner harmony of body and soul." An effort is made to apply nonviolence at all levels, for, as Shantidas stresses, one cannot demonstrate nonviolence in public if one has not yet achieved it in the privacy of one's own home. It is always a question of inner preparation and strength. The Companions of the Ark take vows of nonviolence and dedication to truth, vows of purification, poverty, service, work, responsibility, co-responsibility, and obedience. These vows are renewed each year.

In 1953 the community moved to Bollène, and ten years later

they set up their home at La Borie Noble, 2000 acres of mountainous farmland in the Cévennes. At the present time, there are two communities of families living there, working on the land, spinning, weaving, and carving. There are now also offshoots of the Ark in Morocco, Belgium, Canada, and Argentina. Living in each community, apart from the Companions who have taken vows, there are novices and young people who are interested in the aim of the order and have come to train for short periods. In addition, throughout France there are Friends of the Ark, who are sympathetic toward the order and organize nonviolent seminars and campaigns. In February 1958, a separate organization, Nonviolent Civic Action, was set up to unite people of differing views within the movement who are dedicated to nonviolent political action.

In 1958, ten years after the Ark's inception, thirty Companions and novices went to Paris; together they fasted, chained to the railings around the obelisk in the Place de la Concorde, to show their determination to end the atrocities being committed in Algeria by both the French army and the Algerian rebels. From that time on, the Companions have demonstrated continually against torture, against internment camps, for the right to conscientious objection, and, of course, against the Bomb. This book is an account of their campaigns and a collection of discourses that Shantidas has given on the subject of nonviolence, showing how simple it is in thought and deed, and how fundamental to the dignity of man.

PART ONE

DEFINITIONS OF
NONVIOLENCE

I

ACTIVE NONVIOLENCE

SUBTLE SIMPLICITY

Nonviolence is something simple but subtle.

It is difficult to put into practice and even to grasp, being completely foreign to our ordinary habits. This problem becomes insurmountable when we *think* we understand—when we think that, obviously, nonviolence consists in the refusal to participate in any struggle whatever and in prudently keeping out of danger.

Nonviolence is essentially three things:

> The Solution of Conflict
> The Force of Justice
> The Lever of Conversion

THE SOLUTION OF CONFLICT

What strikes one immediately about the first definition is that one can only speak of nonviolence if there is conflict and that one cannot call nonviolent someone who tries to preserve his own safety when the world about him is at strife. The man who leads a sheltered life is *perhaps* nonviolent, but it is impossible to tell. One can only be sure of his nonviolence if, the day a conflict breaks out, he settles it without resorting to force or trickery.

For nonviolence means saying No to violence and, above all, to violence in its most violent forms—injustice, abuse, and lying.

Now, in the presence of conflict, what attitudes are possible? At the outset, four spring to mind.

The first is to look away and avoid the whole business, especially if we are not being attacked directly, since "we are always brave enough to put up with other people's misfortunes" (Chamfort). After all, it's none of our business. We stay out of it; or, as a matter of fact, we don't even stay at all—we slip quietly away.

The second attitude is to rush boldly into the fray, to give as good as we get, and twice as good if we can.

The third is to take to our heels and run for cover.

The fourth is to raise our hands, fall on our knees, beg for mercy, invoke Augustan clemency—in short, give in.

Can you see a possible fifth attitude?

THE FIFTH AND LAST RESORT

The fifth attitude possible is nonviolence. This attitude excludes the other four.

I repeat: Nonviolence excludes the other four.

It excludes neutrality
    excludes fighting
    excludes flight
    excludes capitulation.

Do you see?

"Yes, we see, but we are puzzled. For if we must neither fight nor *not* fight, nor run away, nor give in, what are we to do?"

I understand your bewilderment, but the answer is in the

textbook and the textbook is easily found. You need only thumb through it and look for the page. The textbook is called the New Testament.

And what does the New Testament say about legitimate self-defense, about the punishment of thieves and scoundrels, about the honor of "our country," about the safeguarding of Christian civilization—and about all the other good and noble reasons and imperatives for waging a just war and for slaughtering our neighbor with a perfectly tranquil conscience?

> But I say unto you, That ye resist not evil: but whosoever shall smite thee on thy right cheek, turn to him the other also.
>
> And if any man will sue thee at the law, and take away thy coat, let him have thy cloak also.
>
> And whosoever shall compel thee to go a mile, go with him twain.
>
> MATTHEW 5:39–41

Right! Now you see, because it's perfectly clear. And you know the words of the gospel by heart, for you are Christians, or at least there are Christians among you, and you have always lived among Christians.

So I conclude that that is exactly what you do; that you never do otherwise; that you have never seen a Christian do otherwise.

For whoever does otherwise is not a Christian.

It is not I who say so: it is Christ.

"If you love those who love you, greet those who greet you, lend money to those who will give it back to you (with a small percentage), what do you do more than the heathen do?"

So there is no doubt about it: you turn the other cheek.

And immediately it becomes apparent that in so doing, you do not remain neutral. You hit and threaten nobody. You neither flee nor shirk. You stand your ground, you hold your enemy, and you do not let him go until the dispute is settled.

So you have actually found the fifth thing to do—such a new, original, and daring thing that it takes people aback!

And now it remains to explain to them why you do it.

They find it hard to understand. They might very well think, in their bewilderment, that you are slightly perverted and like getting hit twice instead of once.

Smack! on the cheek.

"Hey—don't go yet, sir! You've forgotten something."

"What?"

"That I have two cheeks, sir."

You will have to explain to people why you behave in this way.

You will have to tell them first of all that you have never met a villain hardened enough or sufficiently persevering in his villainy to go on taking advantage indefinitely of the opening given to him and his own impunity. That you have even had the experience of seeing people mad with rage stop as if thunderstruck when you do not retaliate. You will have to explain to them that your reason for behaving like this is that you know your enemy is a man.

A man!

Do you hear? A man!

"You needn't shout! Everybody knows that."

Indeed? *You* know because it's obvious, and above all because you're peacefully seated on a chair.

But in the heat of the fight, when your feelings have carried you away, won't the evidence suddenly appear to prove the contrary? And won't your enemy himself provide you with glaring proof that he is a dangerous beast, a monster, a devil incarnate?

Now, your enemy may very well be frenzied with anger and overpoweringly strong—he will still not be so fierce or hard to overcome as the temptation you will feel to consider him a brute, a monster, and a fiend.

That is the moment—and not now—when you must stick to the hard truth that he is a man—a man like yourself.

If he is a man, the spirit of justice dwells in him as it dwells in you. The spirit of justice dwells in every man, because justice is as simple as two-and-two-make-four.

And two-and-two-make-four for every man, whether he be white, black, yellow, a Papuan or a Frenchman, good, bad, or my enemy. For when two and two are added up, it doesn't depend on my good or bad will, on my knowledge or ignorance, on my strength or skill, that the result should be anything but four.

Now, my cause must be as right as two-and-two-make-four, otherwise nonviolence can do nothing for it.

And this is where we come to the second definition of non-violence: the force of justice.

THE FORCE OF JUSTICE

If you are a defender of justice, as I am ready to believe you are, and as I am sure you want to be, you must ask yourself if there is not such a thing as a force of justice. Make no mistake: what I am saying is a *force of justice*, and not a force applied to the defense of justice and justified for that reason.

Neither am I talking about the strength which combatants draw from the conviction that they are on the side of the just.

I mean a force inherent in justice itself, the "constraining force" I spoke of when I said that two-and-two-make-four.

WHERE THIS FORCE COMES FROM AND ITS INFALLIBLE EFFECTS

The point is, that for two and two to make four, one must equal one.

An axiom common to justice and to mathematics.

Now, everything can be called in doubt, especially tastes and colors, but not the truth of numbers.

The force of justice is that every man is forced to submit to the evidence that one-is-equal-to-one.

Justice is mathematical exactitude in action, the irresistible development of logic and the ineluctable practical result of truth.

But if this is so, how can one explain that there are unjust people? And who is in the wrong?

As a matter of fact, there are no unjust people and nobody is at fault. At least, nobody is unjust and wicked in his own eyes.

To hear people speak, each and every one of us is working and fighting for justice and seeking for good, without which there would be no purpose in our acts nor any motive for action.

But since without goodness and without justice one can get nowhere, failing goodness, we seek a good, and failing justice, we seek a justification.

Evil is not *an* evil, but something partially good taken for total good, an immediate good taken for eternal good.

The contrary of justice is not injustice, but partiality.

Every evil and every injustice begins with an error. "When the thought is wrong, affliction follows as the wheel of the cart follows the step of the bullock," says Buddha (Dhammapada).

One is equal to one: everybody knows that. And so do I—till the *one* in question is myself, for as soon as this enormous unity comes into play, the arithmetic goes wrong and my calculations become muddled.

All the straight lines and all the angles are deviated by original sin and original error.

Who is the villain then? Who is this person who snatches my property from me, tramples my rights underfoot, wants to kill me or those dear to me? The lout! The impudent swine! The disgusting brute! The cold, calculating, treacherous hypocrite, the—in short, my enemy!

What is he?

Just a man who is mistaken.

This discovery is of the highest importance, and on it nonviolence has its foundations.

The first conclusion to draw from it is that I am freed from hating him.

Indeed, it would be useless, ridiculous, out of place, and completely unjust to hate a man because he was mistaken.

The second conclusion is that it is my duty—and my urgent duty—to put him right.

Besides, what could be more natural? Isn't it what we all do—spontaneously—when we hear someone making a mistake, even when he is not talking to us? Even when it is none of our business? Even when it is just a mistake that doesn't matter? And we are right, for the truth is always important, important in itself, important to everybody. Indeed, by truth we live and have our being.

But in this case, it is of prime importance to clear up the misunderstanding, for here lies the cause of conflict and the root of all the trouble.

The third consequence is that my task and my battle lie plain before me like a map: I have to make my enemy's justifications fall one by one—the justifications that defend, encircle, and blind him—until such time as he stands naked and alone, face to face with his own judgment.

Truth will get the better of him.

Whereupon I shall have found a way of settling the conflict.

THE FORCE OF PERSUASION

That's easily said, and highly satisfying, but let us beware of thinking that the conflict can be settled as by the touch of a magic wand.

I have said that nonviolence is a simple thing: I am not saying that it is easy.

It is already good to know that nonviolence is possible and to get people to admit as much.

Even if nonviolence can only be achieved at the price of fatigue, suffering, and above all, thought—it costs less than violence. Moreover, it does not entail defeat, humiliation, or revenge. It is wisdom, and wisdom is a great saving of suffering and crime.

Sometimes nonviolence nips conflict in the bud, appeasing by dignified, kind, and equitable words the adversary who has lost his temper because he believes himself ill-used, insulted, or in danger. That is what is meant by the force of persuasion.

THE FORCE OF CONVICTION

But sometimes speech is action, more powerful and real than any other action.

I shall take an example from the life of David.

King David, as you know, had taken the wife of one of his soldiers and then sent the brave man off to be killed.

Everything was going well when who should come up to the king's room but the Prophet, to appeal to him about a lamentable case.

"There is a poor man," said the Prophet, "who had only one ewe lamb, and he loved it. A rich neighbor envied him his white ewe and, by treachery, not only stole it but also set an ambush for the man and had him done to death!"

"Oh! whoever is this scoundrel?" cried David indignantly. "Bring him here and have him judged and sentenced to death!"

But the Prophet, looking him in the face and pointing at him, said, "The scoundrel is yourself!"

It was done. At once David understood. He fasted, and wept, and "lay all night upon the earth."

But one does not always have to deal with a scoundrel of David's kind. Generally, it takes more to touch a man's conscience.

It would nevertheless be a prejudice to think of anyone: "This person is so vile, so brutal, that he will never understand any other language than that of force."

The life of prisoners-of-war in Germany was hard, what with cold, hunger, forced labor, and the nightly return to their huts. For the booted guard used to wait for them so that he could work off his feelings on them in ways that amused nobody but himself. He would pull one man's nose, kick another in the belly, and so on; and each of them would wonder whether that night it would be *his* turn.

This went on until one evening a prisoner stepped forward and said, "Since you *have* to bully someone every day, pick on me this time."

"Ha! ha! little Frenchy!" sneered the guard. "Since you're so clever, tell me how often you're going to feel my whip on your—"

"It's not for me to say how often I deserve it: I leave that to your conscience!"

"My conscience! My conscience! But I haven't got a conscience!"

There was a silence, then the prisoner said, "Yes, you have, and the proof is that you haven't struck me yet."

He calmly walked off a few paces and then, without looking at him, added, "I don't even believe you'll hit me tonight . . ."

Then he looked around.

The German was staring in front of him, pale, with his eyes full of tears and his lips trembling.

Nobody had ever spoken to the poor brute of his conscience and perhaps that was the reason for his brutishness.

From that day onward, he never struck a prisoner. The story is so unlikely that I wouldn't tell it if it weren't true.[1]

THE POWER OF ACCEPTED SUFFERING

Let us come back to the Bible and the man struck on the cheek, for we are now in a better position to understand what the point is. What does "Turn the other cheek" mean? It means: "Get your enemy to do you twice as much harm as he intended." Why?

Because the man who struck you unjustly somehow knows that it was unjust, or at least in his inner depths someone knows, a someone he does his best to smother. The spirit of justice hidden in his depths expects the blow to be returned. He needs it —it would justify the one he gave you and enable him to keep the hostilities going.

Now, instead of getting the slap he is expecting, he is, on the contrary, going to be led into putting himself doubly, triply, quadruply in the wrong.

Here is a rule of nonviolent tactics: lead and force the enemy into multiplying his misdeeds.

As for you, bear them with patience, with constancy and hope.

Wait without flinching until he has done enough wrong and injustice for something to stir in his obscure soul.

THE LEVER OF CONVERSION

And here we are at the heart of the matter: the conversion of the enemy is not a means of attaining our end, but the real object of nonviolence. However good, desirable, and just the results we are aiming at—compensation for the harm done, expiation of the offense, the achievement of freedom, security, and

---

[1] Jean Goss told me this story as if he had only witnessed it, but I suspect him of being the hero, it is so much in keeping with his character.

peace—these are not our real object. Our real object is the changing of the enemy into a friend, of the wicked man into a just man, of the tyrant into a fair-minded and generous ruler. What follows will only be the result and one of the consequences of the harmony achieved.

But if one seeks agreement and wins the adversary's good graces only as a means of obtaining one's ends, then one is using cleverness, praiseworthy no doubt, but quite different from nonviolence.

Getting what we want out of the adversary, not because he has come around to our way of thinking, but because he is afraid of scandal, for example, or because we have made a nuisance of ourselves, is not nonviolence, but what is known as blackmail.

And the most ignoble of all forms of blackmail is speculation on pity, on religious scruples, on the sense of duty or on other good feelings. The jealous woman who aims a revolver at her lover is a mere child compared with the one who threatens to let herself die.

How can one tell whether a man is nonviolent? By his smiles and gentleness? Or because he always says Yes?

Not at all!

By his patience, then? His imperturbable calm?

No! For to be nonviolent it is not enough not to be violent. Nonviolence aims at the conscience.

When calm alone is likely to prick the conscience of a furious adversary, the nonviolent man will astonish him by his humble serenity. When shouting, denunciation, and blows are more likely to shake people out of their inertia, he will find enough courage to be angry.[2]

---

[2] See the author's comment on Jesus and the merchants in the temple in his book *Commentaire de l'Évangile* (Commentary on the Gospels), Paris: Denoël, Chapter 25.

He is capable of mockery and provocation when he sees that his adversary is in danger of mistaking the respect he shows him for flattery, or in danger of loosening his grip out of mere pity.

He is capable of aggression. Whereas violence is made somewhat legitimate by defense, nonviolence is at its purest and most legitimate when it is not defensive. The nonviolent fighter premeditates his attack and takes the road, the boat, or the train to the place where the atrocity or abuse is being practiced and, in order to bear witness to nonviolence and raise his protest, he will create a disturbance or a scandal.

The right way to serve, honor, and save your enemy is to fight him.

And you shall pursue the fight right to the end, the end which is neither victory nor spoil, but reconciliation.

We can now be more precise in our definitions. First, nonviolence is the solution to conflict.

I say *the* solution because there are no others.

Because, if you return evil for evil, you are not putting an end to evil, you are doubling it.

How can you call the evil you are returning "good"?

If, to punish a murderer, you kill him, you are not giving life back to his victim. That only makes two dead men instead of one; and two murderers—he and you.

How can you say it is a lesser evil since *your* justice demands a punishment equal to the crime?

How can you believe it is a way of stopping evil when you are adding a link to which other links will be added?

For the defeated bide their time and take their revenge.

If you kill a man, his brother will avenge him.

If you reduce him to subjugation, you will find yourself at the other end of the rope he is tied with.

Violence breeds violence. Whoever thinks he can free himself by it forges his own chains.

The chains of legitimate violence are stronger and better made than any others.

Nonviolence is the only, the one and only effective solution, a breaking of the chain and liberation.

Even if the enemy is so wily and tenacious that you cannot get the better of him, the struggle will force you into victories over yourself, into inner experiences and discoveries which will bear their fruit.

IN PRAISE OF FORCE

We said that nonviolence is the force of justice.

And thus two things which are too often confused in common opinion are disassociated—force and violence.

Force is the best of things. Force is the value of a being. In Latin, force is called virtue. The plenitude of force, the all-forceful, is God.

Nothing good can come out of weakness, inertia, inaction.

Nothing good can come out of violence, which is the abuse of force, and the abuse of the best is the worst.

Violence is the power of evil in all its forms:

> Brutality or stupid domination by inferior power
> Abuse or violation of the law
> Lying or violation of truth

It is obvious that violence or an excess of force cannot be ended by an excess of the same nature coming from the opposite direction. On the contrary, this only provokes and aggravates it.

It is equally clear that it cannot be made up for by weakness or cowardice. On the contrary, violence, weakness, and cowardice go hand in hand. The violent find great numbers of weak and cowardly people—their strength lies in their numbers—to serve and pay tribute to them. And this combination of violence with weakness and cowardice, consolidated by the rational and moral structure I shall deal with later, ensures the docility of citizens and the discipline of armies.

The only force that can oppose violence is, therefore, the force of justice.

THE TWO POWERS

"There are two powers in the world, the power of the sword and the power of the spirit. The power of the spirit will always, in the end, conquer the power of the sword."

If you think this is how some great spiritual leader, prophet, or teacher sees history, you are mistaken.

It is how Napoleon saw it.

It was the role of another hero to prove it true, a hero innocent of his brothers' blood—Gandhi.

And it is straight from the epic of his life[3] that the word "nonviolence" has come into our language, a translation of the Sanskrit *Ahimsa*. But Gandhi felt the need to give it a stronger and more positive name:

Satyagraha

or "strong adherence to *Sat*, the inner power of *Sat*." Now *Sat* means truth and being. The exact translation is consequently "power of truth" or, to speak like Napoloen, "power of the spirit."

However, one should not think that nonviolence is an invention of Gandhi's. Five centuries before Christ, Buddha was teaching it, and five centuries before Buddha, Joseph, in Genesis.

Neither should one consider nonviolence as something Oriental, of which *we* are incapable. Nonviolence has a long history in the West, and one of its exploits is nothing less than the

---

[3] In *Les Quatre Fléaux* (The Four Scourges), Paris: Denoël, pp. 46–52, I summed up this epic as briefly as I could in the chapter *"De Trois Miracles Historiques"* (Of Three Historical Miracles), to which I refer the reader. He would also do well to read *The Life of Mahatma Gandhi*, by Louis Fischer (Macmillan, 1962).

establishment of the Christian Church, for it is what one might call "the method of the martyrs." Poland, Hungary, and South America have provided several examples of nonviolent revolution and liberation within the last two centuries and, as you know, nonviolent movements (still too few but growing in number) are arising all over the world.

OF EFFICIENCY

The efficiency of nonviolence no longer requires proof. It has become a frequent topic of writing and conversation. I can in all certainty formulate this general rule: all those who deny or doubt its efficiency have no experience of it, as you may observe. The answer to their criticism is "Go and see before you talk about it!"

It is not the efficiency of nonviolence I want to talk about, but the value of efficiency.

"Efficiency" is a word which produces a strange and magical effect upon our contemporaries. So much so that if one could get public opinion to admit that nonviolence is efficient, it would be adopted immediately and wholeheartedly and become customary behavior. Now, it is desirable, urgent, and of capital importance that it should. But if such a happy state of affairs were to come about, it might be only as a result of a misunderstanding. Let us be quite sure there is no misunderstanding, even at the risk of losing the efficiency it might have.

Efficiency is the value of a means quite apart from the value of its purpose.

Thus, technology, economy, strategy, politics, and science are all good in their way.

Technology is efficient for producing all kinds of objects, apart from any consideration of their nature or the use they will be put to, for they may just as easily be tools as weapons, or remedies as poisons, at the service of happiness or of death.

Technology is efficient for speeding up traffic, as distinct from the question of whether it is a good thing to rush without knowing toward what, and whether it is desirable to shorten life by universal hurrying.

Economy is efficient for increasing wealth, apart from any consideration of whether wealth brings happiness or corruption and trouble.

Strategy is efficient for winning battles, quite apart from the cause for which the fighting is being done, or the question of whether there is any cause which justifies the destruction of so many human lives.

Politics is efficient for conquering and keeping power, disregarding the question of whether such power can be for the common good.

Science is efficient for putting into man's hands the mighty forces of nature, setting aside all question of whether it is good that man should be able to bring about outrageous upheavals at will.

But let us now consider whether we have the right to set these questions aside, whether we have the right to devote ourselves entirely to the development of the means and to leave it till some other time and to someone else to think about the ends.

Is not the dissociation of the end and the means a refusal to think and an act of willful blindness? Is it not this dissociation which has led our civilization astray and taken the meaning out of life?

All the things which are valued because of their efficiency belong to the category of means. All these things with their necessities and mechanisms have a value which is relative, secondary, practical, and not to be confused with the religious and moral values which are absolute, primordial, and applicable only to free personal behavior.

But as these secondary values acquire more and more importance in the lives of civilized people for whom they are an ever-increasing means of dominating their neighbors, they come to be considered as superior, and finally as supreme values.

Now, evil is nothing but a partial good taken for Good. This is how things which would be relatively good in their place become an evil in the absolute and an evil in practice, as the periodic return of great scourges like war clearly shows. It is not difficult to see how the usurping secondary values prepare the way for these scourges, bring them about and serve to inflict them.

The degradation of moral values is the counterpart of this idolatry of practical values, above all where collective self-esteem is set up as a virtue and the interest of the group as morality.

Crimes such as homicide, enslavement, deception, corruption, and the exploitation of others are then judged as "means" and justified by their success.

And so one arrives at the too-well-known formula: "The end justifies the means."

The efficiency of nonviolence is that it destroys these justifications which are all based on the false absolutes of technology, politics, strategy, economy, and science.

Nonviolence is the opposite of the justification of evil means by good ends. It is the fitting of the means to the end, and if the end is just, the means must be so too.

Gandhi teaches us that the means and the end are in the same relationship as the acorn and the oak it grows into.

And that the mischief introduced into an undertaking by the means must necessarily subsist in the end.

Which explains the disappointment that comes on the heels of every victory or liberation obtained by violence, even when the cause was good and the combatants heroic and sincere.

No! Good causes do not justify evil means, but evil means spoil the best causes.

One must distinguish between instrumental efficiency and ultimate efficiency.

Science can lend itself to any use: the conscience cannot.

Intelligence can lower itself to any scheme: wisdom cannot.

Power can stoop to anything: self-control cannot.

Money can be put to all kinds of uses: honesty cannot.

Courage can defend any cause: charity cannot.

Power can be used for any purpose, but nonviolence or the power of justice can serve only justice.

IN PRAISE OF JUSTICE

Justice, which is justness, or better still, in Gandhi's words, truth.

Justice, which is truth in action.

Justice is the first of the virtues, without which the others lose their value and become faults.

Justice is the evidence of kindness.

Justice is the law of life and the reason of harmony.

Justice puts everything in its place and keeps it there, each thing being good in its time and place.

Low things being good below for their strength, high things being good above for their clarity.

Pain being good at the proper time of purification, death being good at its hour for deliverance.

Shade being good for rest, fire being good like beauty.

Nothing is worthless, nothing is vile, nothing is false, nothing is foul, nothing is bad but disorder.

Justice is good, like music.

THE TWO JUSTICES

But we know of two justices—true justice, and the other.

True justice returns good for good and multiplies good; returns blessings measure for measure, and for measureless blessings gives thanks; gives to each his due, honor to the great, help to the weak, pity to the small; encourages those who keep to the right path, restrains those who cannot control themselves, brings back those who go astray, raises up those who fall.

The other justice is that which returns evil for evil in order to put an end to evil, but which itself ends in evil and reinforces it; which, in the art of discovering and pursuing the guilty, resorts to every kind of mischief, of sordid villainy and deceit; which, in the art of dealing out vengeance, practices all the delays, all the sidetracking, and all the calculations of the coldest and most inhuman cruelty; which, in the art of increasing suffering, employs all the most appalling refinements; which hangs, burns, tortures with red-hot pincers, suffocates, skins, crushes, tears, gouges out eyes, cuts off hands, twists limbs, impales, castrates, lays bare the entrails and probes them; which brands, degrades, exhibits, vilifies, damns, and kills the soul with the body; which, by its laws, trials, and resources, verdicts and executions, arms the fears and angers of the human beast with all the powers of the systemizing spirit.

Do you understand now the obscure and terrible words of St. Paul: "The law is the power of sin"?

And do you see now what a long way justice has to travel from the law of "an eye for an eye" to reach what St. James calls the law of liberty? (James 2:12)

Now do you understand why Christ *had* to be condemned in in due form and crucified between two thieves, and what an exposure of "human justice" the cross is?

As for you, good people, do you want to know which justice you belong to?

Judge for yourselves; put yourselves on the right or the left!

When you hear of a crime that outrages you, what course do your thoughts take?

Do you wonder what punishment fit for the crime will be inflicted on the criminal, since death is too good for him?

Or else, since justice requires equality, do you reflect on what good you can bring about to compensate for such a great evil? And do you wonder what you could say or do to the wretched criminal to enable him to take himself in hand and redeem himself?

All the generous men and women who, within the last two centuries, have campaigned against interrogation, torture, public executions, the pillory, hard labor, and the death penalty; who have campaigned for the cleaning up and humanizing of prisons, the reeducation of delinquent youth, the welcoming and rehabilitation of freed prisoners, the respect of those under arrest, probation for those who have committed their first offenses, and partial freedom for deserving prisoners; all those people who, to their great credit, have discovered by themselves and in the face of the hostility of the rest of the world this glaring evidence: the horror of repressive justice—all those are to be numbered among the champions of nonviolence, even if they do not use the word.

THE INEVITABLE CONSEQUENCES
OF REPRESSIVE JUSTICE

Now, repressive justice, and what it involves, is the backbone of our secular institutions.

Our judges in ermine and our bemedaled governors understand no other justice. The prosperity of our businesses, the coziness of our family life are founded on it.

Let us not be surprised, then, if Jesus reveals on the last day of his life that the Spirit will convict the world of "sin, justice, and judgment" and that "the Prince of this World has already been judged" (paraphrase, John 16:8–11).[4]

---

[4] For the Prince of this World is the prisoner of the laws he has made and the victim of the violence he has brought about. He suffers from the fear and hatred he himself has created. What is meant by Christ is that by his own verdict, the Prince of this World is excluded from all love, from all truth, and

But if one wants to understand how the world is condemned for its sin, justice, and judgment, one must consider not only what violent justice involves in the normal course of events, but also the form that lawful violence takes when it is unleashed.

What is meant by "the unleashing of lawful violence"?

War!

And note that we are speaking of lawful violence, for unlawful violence, that which springs from hatred, jealousy, envy, greed, anger, and other wickedness, is the business of morals, but nonviolence attaches very little importance to it.

It grieves me when I read in the headlines that a man who has killed two or three others has been arrested, that he is going to be tried and will perhaps be hanged.

Whereas I feel like running to congratulate him on killing so few people—only two or three! Poor man!

In the meantime, those who are manufacturing death for all of us with their bomb at Marcoule or Aldermaston or elsewhere—those who are preparing leprosy for millions of innocent beings, some of them not yet born—are in no danger whatever of being hanged!

They are honorable citizens. Wealth is lavished on them in proportion to their disinterested science, and honors heaped on them for the good they are doing to humanity.

And the decent men, the workers, the employees, not forgetting the cleaners, who devote their waking hours, their thoughts, and their trouble to this marvel of technology and other equally useful work—*their* consciences are clear!

So much so that they even have their trade unions and are not only socialists but pacifists as well. Pacifists who do not bleat but roar, always ready to shout for peace at meetings and demonstrations.

---

from all justice, and he is judged by that verdict; he has already been judged. *Commentaire de l'Évangile,* Chapter 27.

And when everything blows up, it will certainly be somebody else's fault!

And what about ourselves? Are we going to continue, like them, to "carry out our professional duties" without asking ourselves any questions?

When everything blows up, and everything has been going so well until then, shall we explain it by the greed of the gun merchants, or the ambition of the dictators, or the mad hatred and ferocity of the enemy?

No, none of these is required for everything to blow up.

But if each of us continues to perform his professional duty, obeying his boss's orders without asking any questions, that will be quite enough to cause the explosion.

Then we shall have the outbreak of lawful violence or the war of justice.

What need have you, patriots, philosophers, and theologians, to elaborate a doctrine of just war, to prove to us that the most just of wars is the one we are waging!

We know that! Otherwise we would never wage it! Without a good cause and a good reason, nobody would fight.

The reason why animals don't wage war is that they cannot reason, and that they don't know what justice is.

Reason is what arms man for war.

Reason and his spirit of justice supply him with his motives for war.

It is not enough to say that our war is just—we must be convinced that the cause is justice itself and that we are backed up by the very spirit of justice.

What? You don't believe it?

Do you take us for liars? or perhaps for rascals, wrongdoers, murderers? But such riff-raff are incapable of fighting a war! War is not waged with bad feelings: war requires courage, discipline, devotion, and intelligence. It's decent people like us who fight wars.

So we are not liars. But you say we are being misled? Who is misleading us? Our government? Not at all, for once we are in agreement with it!

You say we are being forced into it?

Is it by the force of an army that we are compelled to fight? —we who are armed and could overcome anyone who tried to force us? Is it for interested motives, as some economists say? No, for though they are very knowing, they know nothing of the working of the human heart and nothing—so it seems—of business either.

For if it is to defend interests, why do poor people fight as well as rich? To defend other people's interests? Or to get rich by selling their own skins? Do you really take them for fools?

And as for us, ordinary citizens careful with our money, do you think we are stupid enough to go to war for motives of interest? The interest of each and all of us is that there should be people producing and earning their daily bread, not that we should have an army destroying and devouring everything!

Our interest is the safety of the roads, the opening-up of frontiers, friendship between neighboring peoples, in short, peace.

For it is not the soldiers who pay for war, even when they win it, nor the government, whatever people may think! It is we who pay for it.

As for the disappointments, the damage, the danger—we know they are immense, immediate, and certain, whereas for every one of us the advantages are both uncertain and far distant.

Again, even if we are eager for gain, we are still more attached to our lives and those of our children, and no amount of wealth can protect anyone from the dangers of war.

Is hatred the motive then?

I've never seen the enemy: how could I hate him? And yet,

the fact is, I do hate him, for I hate everything he represents. I don't hate him spontaneously, but I make it my duty to hate him out of my love for justice. For he represents the spirit of evil. He is the incarnation of the spirit of evil. He is force against right, barbarism against civilization, slavery against freedom. It is he who is the wrongdoer, and God is with me!

All these reasons are irrefutable, and such is our sincerity that we are ready to affirm them even if it costs us our lives.

And so is the enemy.

War is the spirit of justice raised to a frenzy. What can be more exalting than to be the accuser and at the same time the judge and the executor of the punishment?

Sin, justice, and judgment: "already judged!"

At this crucial point in history, the Tree of the Knowledge of Good and Evil puts forth its finest fruit.

The tree whose root is cunning, whose sap is rivalry, whose boughs are technology, economy, strategy, politics, science. And at the trunk where these boughs join, the fruit: The Bomb. Do you hear me?

Or have you ears but hear not?

Even if you have no wisdom, is there any common sense left in your head? And even if you have no love in your heart, is there not just enough animal fear in you to make you face the one and only issue? The issue which presents itself at precisely this historical hour? Accidentally, you think?

Have you eyes but see not?

But can nonviolence put an end to war?

Read Gandhi's life and you will see that he ended a war in five days, all by himself.

If nonviolence cannot stop war, nothing can stop it, and in Kennedy's words, "either humanity must put an end to war or war will put an end to humanity." The future must therefore be a future of nonviolence, or else there is no future.

But, against a foreigner who takes advantage of our voluntary disarmament and occupies our country, what can nonviolence do?

Once more, ask Gandhi how he expelled a magnificently equipped army of occupation from his country without striking a single blow.

Or, if you dislike always having the same example thrust upon you, ask Commander Stephen King-Hall for his plan of national defense in the nuclear age.[5] This soldier, whose remarkably independent mind and keen pragmatical awareness are enlivened by a spark of English humor, has recognized the fact that good Queen Victoria is dead and that to speak today of armed defense against guided missiles is to reveal an old-fashioned way of thinking.

He describes the tactics by which a people worthy of freedom can stand up to the oppressor, or, to put it more aptly, get the better of him, for Stephen King-Hall is more given to heroic irony in the *Till Eulenspiegel* vein than to tragedy.

But something more than this is needed. The fact is that nonviolence requires a sacrifice almost as big as that required by war, plus twice as much courage. And yet, the history of certain peoples provides us with examples.

Violence does not always shed blood nor is oppression always by a foreigner.

It can take the form of abuse, which is a state of latent and constant violence liable at any moment to break into revolt.

Such is vertical violence[6]—that which the rich practice on the poor, and governors on the governed in order to wring work and taxes out of them within the framework of established order and, of course, according to strictly legal procedures.

[5] S. King-Hall. *Power Politics in the Nuclear Age* (Verry, 1962).
[6] The expression is Bartholomew of Ligt's.

Ask Gandhi how he freed the pariahs[7] and what he meant by *Swadeshi*—economic independence or an economy free of every form of exploitation or oppression of other people.[8]

Ask Vinoba what he means by *Bhoo-Dân* and *Sarvôdaya*,[9] and how he puts them into practice.

Lastly, let us not forget the fact that, whatever Sorel and Marx may say, the strike has not only been the historical instrument of the rise of the worker in the West, but it is the nonviolent weapon *par excellence*. Purified and generalized in the form of noncooperation and nonviolent civil disobedience, it would suffice to bring about the necessary reforms and at the same time contribute to the maturity of the peoples.

Perhaps you are thinking, "There is only one objection to nonviolence, but probably it cannot be overcome, and that is that it presupposes the complete knowledge of truth, and no one knows truth."

That truth is nobody's exclusive possession is itself a truth and one that the nonviolent must never lose sight of. This is all the more reason for practicing nonviolence; first, lest we be mistaken, and then, if we are right, so that we may make of the struggle and the preparation for the struggle an instrument for increasing our knowledge of truth.

Frenzied insistence on being right is the most characteristic feature of lawful violence. In fact, it is an uncontrollable passion.

It is accompanied by the conviction that the enemy is not only bad and of bad faith, but that he is evil itself, and that getting rid of him is the only means of getting rid of the evil.

The error is so gross that it seems improbable that even a

---

[7] Lanza del Vasto. *Return to the Source* (Schocken, 1972).

[8] A capitalist economy practices exploitation and oppression; a communist economy eliminates exploitation but increases oppression.

[9] Lanza del Vasto. *From Gandhi to Vinoba: The New Pilgrimage* (Schocken, 1974).

fool should fall into it, but even the most intelligent people are taken in by it as soon as their anger gets the better of their judgment. And whole peoples suddenly judge whole peoples in this way, and there you have the crazy reason for wars.

So the frontier between good and evil is the frontier between us and them! This is what one may indeed call simplemindedness.

What we must get into our heads and never forget is that the frontier between good and evil passes right through the center of everything.

Right through the middle! between the right and the left!

The fundamental postulate on which the whole of nonviolence depends is, as we have seen, that the spirit of justice dwells in my enemy as it dwells in me. And the complement of this postulate is that evil and error dwell in me as in him.

By admitting that there is good in him, in spite of my anger urging me to the contrary, I detach him from the evil into which my anger wants to plunge him.

By admitting that there is evil in me which my pride refuses to see, I detach myself from my anger and my pride and come nearer to the heart of justice.

Thereupon it is no longer my enemy that I hate, but the evil in him.

"For we wrestle not against flesh and blood," says St. Paul, "but against principalities, against powers, against the rulers of the darkness of this world, against spiritual wickedness in high places," and he speaks of the fight against "those who walk according to the course of this world, according to the Prince of the power of the air."

What holds my attention in this saying is, among other things, the word "Prince." Not an evil, not a devil, but *the Prince of the power of the air.*

For, as we know, evil is always a partial good. My enemy's error is a truth, perhaps a highly elevated truth, which prevents him from seeing the truth, a justification which is taking the place of justice.

Fatherland, honor, right, freedom are brilliant things which have their place neither on earth nor in heaven. They "dwell in the air," they are out of this world, and for them, brother fights brother and we forget God.

We must not be daunted by our reservations concerning absolute truth. Unworthy as we are, ignorant as we are, we must nevertheless stand up for justice, and that is what will deliver us from unworthiness and our ignorance.

Making out that a cause is absolutely good because it is our cause is one thing, and adopting a cause because it is good is another.

Like all mortals, we can make mistakes. We must take this danger into account in our actions, and if we are entirely humble and sincere, it will come about that, contrary to all that might be foreseen, our very fallibility will turn to our advantage.

In the conflict we are involved in, let us ask ourselves what our share of the blame is.

There is no doubt that we are to blame, for, if we were sinless, there would be no conflict. The *Yog-Sutras* teach that "the state of nonviolence having been attained, violence collapses in the presence of the sage." The struggle will be all the harder as we are the less pure. But the tribulations we shall have to suffer at the hands of the unjust will not be so unjust as they seem. If we know this, they will be good for us.

When we have discovered what our fault is, instead of behaving like our enemy and hiding it, instead of imprisoning ourselves in our justifications and reinforcing him in his, we shall confess our mistake and, with disarming simplicity, offer to make up for it in order to break the circle and encourage the enemy to turn in upon himself.

If we accuse the enemy, he will answer reasons with insults and accusations with accusations. But if it is ourselves we accuse, he will listen and follow us. Henceforth, it is we who lead the battle, and we have laid a mine under his fortifications, that is to say, his justifications.

But the value of my cause is quite independent of the merits or faults of whoever defends it. It is the objective value of this cause that I must first be sure about and this requires profound reflection. It is on this objective value that I depend, not on my own strength. The value of the cause is what my action must make evident, and my action must be in conformity with the nature of the conflict and in proportion to its gravity. It must be such that by the choice of the place, the time, the manner and the style of its manifestation, it shall become a symbol.

But so as not to impair the nobility of my cause, and to safeguard it from my weakness, the least I can do is *not to behave like my enemy*: not to put the defender of right in the wrong. . I must at all costs avoid committing the violence, the trickery and offenses I reproach him with.

There is no spiritual exercise more difficult, more efficacious, than this.

In nonviolence, without fighting against myself, I can gain no victory whatever over the enemy.

If there is evil in me as in my enemy, and if it is only the evil I am opposed to, it follows that I must do things in the proper order and begin by fighting the evil in myself.

How can I convert the other man if I myself am not sufficiently converted?

How can I drive his fault home to him and make his justification fall if I allow him to make use of this false but crushing justification: the possibility of his saying to me, "And what about yourself?"

The first blow to strike against the evil in me is to recognize it, and sometimes this single blow is enough to deliver me.

I cannot set myself up as a judge until I have at least begun to purify myself.

"The battlefield of nonviolence," says Vinoba, "is the heart of man." So is the field of maneuvers.

The proper preparation for nonviolence is initiation into inner life, that is to say, knowledge, possession, and giving of oneself.

That is why the Ark[10] exists, in order to begin at the beginning (and from childhood, for those who are born there). The beginning is to establish it in the secret of one's heart, then to practice it within the circle of one's closest acquaintances, and, finally, to try one's hand at civic action.

But if, moved by other people's trouble and suffering, or outraged by some scandal, your generosity has carried you straightaway into a public demonstration, there is no need to worry too much about your lack of spiritual background and training, as long as you put yourself into the hands of a good leader. Experience will soon make you realize the need for inner preparation, and he who seeks, finds.

Anything is better than to excuse yourself with a trite remark such as, "Nonviolence is for saints, and I'm no saint."

The point is to be a man.

"Violence," says Gandhi, "is the law of the brute, nonviolence is the law of man."

By giving in to the law of the brute—the brute armed with intelligence—man brings about the deadening of his spirit and his ultimate destruction.

It is a question of being a man and saving your life—to give your life in order to save Life.

---

[10] The name of the community founded by the author.

2

NONVIOLENCE
AND SELF-DEFENSE

A friend: "Supposing I'm attacked by a bandit at night and put up what defense I can, and I happen to kill him, would I be utterly condemned by the law of nonviolence?"

Shantidas: "No. Probably all those who fight are guilty of the sin 'of which the sting is death,' but to different degrees.

"We don't put a man who kills in order to defend his life when he has been taken by surprise and doesn't know what to do in the same category as the man who has attacked in order to rob him.

"We don't class bandits and soldiers under the same heading, as some people do, even though there is a great similarity between them.

"And when peoples are at war, we don't consider that their causes are exactly equivalent if one of them is waging war in order to subjugate and crush, whereas the other is fighting to recover its freedom, even if each is guilty of numberless crimes."

A war-resister: "I find your answer extremely disappointing, not to say shocking; I thought that in the doctrine of nonviolence I had at last found a firm stand and unevasive answers, and here we are trotting out all the old, outworn arguments of the just war and legitimate self-defense.

"But you know better than anybody else that defense and attack are the two sides of the same picture, and that the argument cuts both ways. You know that *everybody* is always 'defending himself,' including the aggressor. You know that 'the best form of defense is to attack first,' and you know the rest of the story. People will go on arguing about it till the Bomb puts an end to the arguing and the fighting, because there will be nobody left to argue or fight!"

Shantidas: "Nonviolence is simple and primordial, not half-baked and undiscriminating.

"If things were as clear as you believe them to be, so many great minds, and saints among them, would not have found them so confusing or been so self-contradictory on the subject. The absolute is what we are striving for, but in human affairs 'for' and 'against' are intertwined and we cannot—I regret— make sweeping statements."

The war-resister: "But if you grant somebody the right to kill in order to defend himself, how does he differ from anybody else? For that's exactly what the most violent of the violent do."

Shantidas: "I don't grant him the right or else I refuse him the title of nonviolent, but I don't look upon him as a murderer either."

The war-resister: "But I can't see how nonviolence differs from ordinary morals, then, according to your distinction."

Shantidas: "In this, that we consider the circumstances invoked as extreme, exceptional, and overpowering, and that in such circumstances 'necessity knows no law.' But we shall beware of formulating a general rule on the basis of this very special case and we shall be careful not to draw any conclusion or deduction from it concerning legitimacy.

"In actual fact, most human conflict takes place in quite another manner. Most of it, if not all of it, can be solved in a humane fashion. But striking whoever has hit, killing whoever has killed, or tried to kill, or might want to try—that's not a humane solution: it's the reaction of the brute.

"Of all solutions, nonviolence is the most humane."

The war-resister: "I understand you better now. Excuse my outburst."

Shantidas: "Your outburst does you honor. Nonviolence does not consist in not making an outburst."

A Companion:[1] "But to come back to the case of the attack at night—what must a nonviolent person do?"

Shantidas: "Raise his hands, but in order to join them and start praying aloud for his aggressor, for if death carries him off at that moment, believe me, he is blessed!

"But perhaps death will avoid him. Perhaps the aggressor will be disconcerted by such strange behavior. Perhaps he will spare himself a useless crime since the main cause of violence is fear. And so the nonviolent man will have saved his life. This was not his aim, but it's quite an appreciable result all the same. My point in saying this is that even on the plane of mere common sense, nonviolence is not so 'soft' as it appears."

A visitor: "Allow me to tell you that you're fooling yourself about people being good at heart, and especially about the goodness of bandits! I'd like to see a greater sense of reality in your teaching, which I admire apart from that."

Shantidas: "Since you mention reality, have you really ever happened to be attacked by bandits at night?"

The visitor: "No, thank God!"

---

[1] A member of the Community of the Ark, who has taken vows.

Shantidas: "I have. Since you prefer reality to reason, perhaps a true story will convince you more readily.

"It happened on the road from Homs to Baalbek, during my pilgrimage to the Holy Land. I had been warned that I would meet bandits or wolves, but the moon was full, the night was beautiful, and I felt drawn by the solitude.

"It wasn't long before I met them, my gang of thieves, lined up at the side of the road. I went up to them without any fear, not out of bravado, but because of that lack of the sense of reality you so rightly reproach me with. As a matter of fact, they looked so like the picture of bandits in storybooks that it was almost funny.

"Anyway, they had soon relieved me of my bag and my stick, tied my hands and pushed me, by means of a gun between my shoulder blades, into the chief's tent, which was hidden in a hollow.

"There, they searched me, but found nothing.

" 'Who are you?'

" 'A pilgrim.'

" 'Where are you going?'

" 'To Jerusalem.'

" 'What do you live on?'

" 'Allah sees to it.'

"From that instant, everything changed. They made me be seated and began questioning me about Christ, Islam, the Alaouites (for that's what they were), and about the Trinity and Unity. They translated the answers for each other and showed pleasure in them.

"Finally, they summoned a woman—a slave or one of their wives—who came in with her tattooed face unveiled. She poured some water out of a ewer onto my hands and feet and gave me rice and sour milk to eat.

"After that, my hosts helped me to put up my little tent beside their big one and wished me good night.

"Shortly afterward, howling broke out on the horizon, the howling of wolves. The men went out with their guns and fired some shots at random, and the great calm fell again.

"I praised God for delivering me from the wolves by means of the band of thieves, and meditated on wolves and men and, unlike some philosophers, inclined toward the latter (for purely subjective reasons, I agree).

"But I couldn't go to sleep, for there was something on my mind: the money I was carrying on me that the thieves hadn't discovered. A friend had sewn it into a lining, saying, 'Just behave as if you hadn't any, but the day you are in dire need you'll be thankful for having such a prudent friend.' It was a small sum, but so far it had been a weight to carry, and now it was burning me. For it falsified the answer that had moved the thief so deeply as to make him change his attitude, the answer that pretended to perfect detachment and total confidence in God.

" 'I really *am* a fool,' I thought, 'to undo my journey and all my footsteps for so little!'

"I tore the money out of its hiding place, tied it up in a handkerchief, and next day, as I was taking leave, handed it to the robber. But he scowled, put his hand on his dagger, and all but threw himself on me. What did I take him for? For someone who wanted to be paid for his hospitality?

"I calmed him down as best I could, but it wasn't easy.

"At last, with a furious gesture, he rammed the money into my pocket, shouting, 'God forbid that I should touch anything belonging to a *hadj*, a *marabout*, a guest!'

"And thereupon followed the ceremony of blessing and farewell."

The visitor: "That's all very nice, but I don't think you would have the same success with a Parisian apache."

Shantidas: "That may be. I'm not maintaining that nonviolence is an infallible recipe for getting you out of holes and winning every time. But is it some unfortunate experience that has given you such a bad opinion of Parisian thieves?"

The visitor: "Oh, no! But I can hardly imagine them being like your noble Syrian Arab, affected by religious respect or indeed any other kind of respect."

Shantidas: "I prefer experience to a 'sense of reality' that belongs to theory or imagination."

The visitor: "What sort of experience do you expect to have with a thief other than being robbed and calling the police? I've had that experience. Surely you're not going to force me to run after the thief with a gift for him?"

Shantidas: "You're all laughing and you think that's funny. But it would be more amusing to try."

The visitor: "You'd need to be a good runner! And have *you* ever tried, apart from Syria?"

Shantidas: "No, but at least something approaching it. One morning, when we were at Tournier,[2] a hefty-looking man turned up, out of breath and disheveled, with his clothes all rumpled. He told us he had been wandering in the woods all night, looking for a house.

"The welcome he got soon made the hunted look disappear from his face. He stayed with us for a week, and during that time he kept us amused—not to say dazed—with stories of his adventures all over the world. But somehow his stories left us uneasy, for we couldn't help feeling that there were others he was keeping quiet.

"So we weren't very surprised when we discovered that our

[2] The name of the estate in Saintonge where the first Community of the Ark was founded.

money, which we kept in a cardboard box in a drawer of the common room, had disappeared, and he with it.

"One of our Companions made an inspection of the room he had occupied, and found a lot of tiny scraps of paper which he managed to piece together. It was a letter which revealed what we presumed to be his name and address.

"The same evening, the Companion took the train for Paris and, at breakfast time, rang the doorbell. The door opened and the big man appeared. He immediately lost his self-composure and broke into muddled explanations and entreaty.

"But the Companion said to him, 'I've come specially from the Community to reassure you about this little incident. We are very happy to have been of some service to you and to have sheltered you from the police who were after you.'

"Whereupon, finding his tongue again, the unfortunate creature poured out thanks, but the Companion cut him short.

" 'Thank God rather for the warning he has sent you at this hour of your destiny. My Companions beg you to take pity on yourself and change your manner of life.'

"We had no more news of our poor scoundrel, and I can't assure you that he became an honest man overnight.

"But what does seem certain to me is that our nonviolent pursuit of him was more likely to put him on the straight path than a trial and three months' imprisonment."

A family man: "Exposing yourself in such a manner to robbery and even murder is all to your credit, but would *I* have the right to endanger my children and my family's property and to prefer my ideas to their lives?"

Shantidas: "Do you think I prefer 'ideas' to life? My ideas— no! my safeguard and my reason for living. As for you, it's either one thing or the other: either you believe in nonviolence and practice it as others practice violence—at the risk of your life and the lives of others, it's all one—or you don't believe in it, and in that case you have no right to risk anyone's life, not even your own, out of curiosity and just to see if it works. (It wouldn't work, by the way.) But in any case, you take good care not to, don't you? Besides, we all know what an excellent excuse 'the children' are, but it's wearing thin."

A lady: "Haven't you yourself written that if putting an end to war meant putting an end to the warlike virtues, war would be preferable?"

The war-resister: "Oh!"

Shantidas: "Just what are the warlike virtues? Courage, discipline, the sense of honor, the spirit of justice, the spirit of sacrifice. Putting an end to these would be killing the soul of man. Yes, in that case, death would be preferable.

"But why are these virtues called warlike? Because they are to be met with even in war and because one is astonished to admire them there, in spite of the evils they bring about.

"But they are admired as virtues, and not as being warlike. They are admired for their beauty, not for their misdeeds.

"They have their place equally, and more appropriately, in peace, whereas in war, every form of cowardice, rapacity, and vileness also has its place.

"But in time of peace, it must be admitted that the noble virtues remain dormant in most men because of the coziness of commodity, the thought-preventing whirl of pleasure, and the calculations of profit-seeking. Fire and the sword wake them up, and thus fighting favors them. But nonviolence is also a fight— a fight for peace in time of war as in time of peace, and it requires a double measure of the warlike virtues."

The war-resister: "What exactly is your position concerning conscientious objection to military service?"

Shantidas: "The army and a perpetual state of readiness for war are unquestionably a sign of the state of sin in which all human society finds itself, and military service is a mark of servitude. The fact that this servitude is more serious in democracies than in any other regime is still another proof that it is not due to the wickedness of those in power, but is a consequence of the common sin.[3]

"The conscientious objector is therefore right in the absolute, but we don't live in the absolute, and neither does he. And among the motives by which he may be inspired, some are excellent, some questionable, some bad, and some very bad.

"What is right, dignified, and opportune is to uphold the first right of man, the right to rise above the passions that citizenship may rouse in him and to obey his conscience rather than to yield to pride, common opinion, and the threats of power. The right to consider the divine commandment: "Thou shalt not kill" as absolute and to act and bear witness accordingly. When a man proves that he prefers being killed to killing, those who persecute him make him a martyr.

"The attitude of the conscientious objector becomes questionable when he is not aware of all the implications of his refusal; when he takes the army for the cause of war, whereas it is only an instrument; when he takes war for an evil in itself and the root of all evil, whereas it is only a result; when he objects to war but doesn't object to any of the things that make war inevitable, and may even earn his living by them.

"The true conscientious objector, that is to say the objector who is fully conscious, objects to a certain peace as well as to war and is against all forms of abuse, excess, and lying that are covered by the law; he is opposed to oppression and exploitation

[3] In *Les Quatre Fléaux* there is a clear analysis of the relationship between original sin and war (as between original sin and other scourges created by man), a relationship which has always been obscurely felt but hitherto nowhere explained.

and to the industrial, commercial, political, police, and legal systems.[4]

"The first act of objection is refusal to cooperate with these systems or to benefit by them; the second is to form a militia of resistance and intervention and to pass from conscientious objection to nonviolent civic action in one way or another.[5]

"But what is to be said of the conscientious objector whose awareness of moral responsibility does not even rise to that of the ordinary citizen, and who refuses obligations and service like the fool who, when a house has caught fire, refuses to help the fire-fighters because his own room is still untouched?

"Lastly, what could be more abject than to refuse to fight for fear of getting hurt! Improbable as it seems,[6] the objector will always be suspected of cowardice until, like his predecessor and patron, St. Martin, he supplies proof to the contrary.

"As you know, Martin, being the son of a veteran of the Roman army, had been compelled to serve in it. But one day he made up his mind to lay down his sword and become a soldier of Christ, even if it were to cost him his life.

"His captain and his companions jeered at him and called him a coward, for the barbarians were expected to attack the following day.

"But the objector replied, 'I'll go into battle, then, but without a sword or armor.'

"And he did so, in the front line.

---

[4] Organizations such as the International Movement of Reconciliation, the War Resisters' International, International Civilian Service, and the Quaker Society of Friends do not limit conscientious objection to war but endeavor to fight war's causes as far as they know them.

[5] Nonviolent Civic Action exists in France. During the last three years of the war in Algeria and since then, it has been campaigning constantly. The address of the Secretariat is La Borie Noble, 34260, Le Bousquet d'Orb, France.

[6] It is highly improbable that a coward would refuse openly, in the face of the whole world. A coward prefers to desert or obtain exemption by simulating illness, worse still, "shooting off his mouth" in the barracks and fleeing or hiding in battle.

"Astonished to see the defenseless rider, the barbarians laid down their arms and asked for peace.

"It is desirable, honorable, and reasonable that a civilized country should admit conscientious objection and should allow objectors to work for the common good instead of languishing in prison.

"That is why we have joined our efforts to yours in order to obtain a statute of conscientious objectors in France. But we have done so without any illusions, for even if we obtained it, the redoubtable problem of war would remain unsolved and a statute would even deprive the act of objection of a part of its significance and efficiency."

Someone: "I've done nothing but be nonviolent all my life, and I'm afraid I must admit that when all's said and done, it hasn't worked."

Shantidas: "That's surprising! How did you set about it? What did you do?"

The same person: "What did I do? That's just it; I didn't do anything—just let myself be had, like an idiot!"

Shantidas: "I shall say nothing."

The man who thinks himself nonviolent: "Why not?"

Shantidas: "Because, if you haven't listened to what I've been saying from the start, what chance is there of my being listened to now?"

3

THE COMMUNITY SOLUTION

OF THE FIRST STEPS

Let us see what the practical solutions are, for time is short. How can the two blocs be prevented from producing new bombs and hurling them at each other over our heads, or perhaps through us?

Time is indeed short. So, as a wise man said, let us be wise enough not to hurry.

Your broadmindedness and self-effacement do you honor. Your first thought is to put world affairs in order, and you have completely forgotten yourself!

Because time is short, beware of taking the three hundred and thirty-third step before you have taken the first: it would be a waste of time.

I ask you: no matter how big-hearted you are, can you give what you haven't got? Before you can spread peace on earth, you must have brought it into your own home, and there can be no peace in your home if there is none in your heart.

Justice and peace cannot be brought into the world without violence and coercion if, on your own and other people's acts, you impose the boundary lines of the law and other rules of the game. Justice is nonviolent and free when action springs from within and its order reflects the order reigning within.

Nonviolence is spoken of as a technique or tactics: it is nothing of the kind, unless in metaphor. It is neither a procedure, nor a recipe, nor a system.

"It is a way of doing which springs from a way of being" (Aldo Capitani).

Justice, as we have seen, is founded on unity and equality. To be more exact: on outer equality and inner unity.

But have you got inner unity? Do you even know what it is? Above all, do you know that you haven't got it?

If my reader feels offended at this rash and random opinion of him, then my words have hit the mark and he should take them to heart, not as an insult, but as an admonition. Whoever possesses inner unity and knows what it is will be unaffected by them, knowing how rare that unity is and how difficult to achieve. He will also know that inner unity cannot be stung by wounded pride.

Your first step, then, is to train for nonviolence. Everybody knows that war takes years of preparation, preparation which requires preparation from childhood onward, at home and at school. Surely peace cannot be won at less expense.

The task is twofold: we must not only learn the new way, but also unlearn the old one that has been dinned into us all our lives long and is exemplified by everything in our environment.

However, in preparation for nonviolence, there is no need for costly apparatus or maneuvers on the training field. We must train with perseverance, sparing no effort, and train in three ways, in secret, in private, and in public.

OF SECRET PREPARATION

By definition, the nature of secret preparation cannot be revealed. Not that it has anything to do with plotting or Black Mass or magic ritual or secret societies with passwords to safeguard their occult privileges.

On the contrary, nothing is by nature simpler or more clear. It is a matter of advancing toward self-knowledge and self-possession with a view to giving oneself; a matter of mental concentration, control of the emotions and senses, bodily training, and a corresponding rule of life.

By right, it is universal and open to all, but cannot be communicated in writing, just as music and fencing cannot be learned from books. It must be transmitted in private; you must ask, be shown how, watched over and protected.[1]

No more can be said here, but secret preparation must be insisted on because of the great number of people who either ignore or forget it. The reason for their failure, however dedicated or willing they may be, is that they have overlooked this essential point.

OF PRIVATE PREPARATION

"Nonviolence is the finest quality of the soul, but it is developed by practice" (Gandhi).

If nonviolence is the art of peacemaking, there is no lack of opportunity for practice, and you can start this very evening, or rather, tomorrow, for sleep brings counsel.

Certainly we are never short of conflict. Almost everybody is on the brink of, or in the heat of some difference with his or her parents or children or wife or husband or employees or employer or hallporter or neighbor, if not with someone or other who has just trodden on his foot or snatched his wallet.

Begin with the simple conflicts which appear to be easily solved. (It won't be as easy as you think.) On the other hand, you will discover that the conflicts to which there was seemingly no possible solution can be solved by nonviolence, and by nonviolence only.

[1] See Lanza del Vasto, *Approches de la Vie Intérieure* (Approaches to Inner Life), Paris: Denoël.

Practice first on people you love and respect and who respect and love you. Before succeeding in loving your enemies, begin by fighting your friends.

Stop quarreling, arguing, and preaching, and fast until your friend understands what, for his own good and for the good of all, he must understand: that such and such an action or gesture is unworthy of him, that he cannot be allowed to commit this or that act of negligence or iniquity. Be patient and calm, and above all, fearless and firm. Don't beat about the bush or dissemble. And go to somebody who can give you advice and encouragement.

OF PUBLIC COMMITMENT

Secret preparation and private preparation will train you for public action, but public action is itself preparation for further public action.

You must not commit yourself without preparation, but neither should you wait to be perfect before beginning, for then you will wait forever, and events don't wait to rush upon us. Moreover, each form of preparation is the field of distinct and specific experiences, so it is best to go ahead with all three at the same time and not one after the other. It will suffice to make your plans according to such strength and clear-sightedness as you possess.

A beginner should not plunge into public action singlehanded unless he has a special vocation. He should look for some well-guided group he can enter. Teachers of nonviolence should be distinguished from soldiers or servants of nonviolence. The former are able to draw on their own resources for a plan of action and the leadership and instruction of their men. Gandhi picked up his collaborators in the street by the thousands, and they trained by following him.

Various movements have arisen in France and tried themselves out in silent demonstration. The Ark has launched the movement of Nonviolent Civic Action and opened training camps. There are also groups of Friends of the Ark in the main towns.

OF THE ARK OR PERMANENT ACTION

But the Ark is engaged in spiritual preparation and in all-round education for nonviolence rather than in any particular public action.

Its interventions have always been signs and testimony rather than undertakings brought to a successful conclusion. The fact is that in order to do, one must first be, and that has been our endeavor. We do not regard spiritual preparation as a means, but as something intrinsically more important than any outer demonstration or victory. Bringing man face to face with God and face to face with himself is what matters and is desirable for its own sake. When the Tree of Life has been found again, our acts will fall from it like ripe fruit full of savor.

Much more than going into the street, distributing tracts, speaking to crowds, knocking on doors, leading walks and campaigns, invading bomb factories, undertaking public fasts, braving the police, being beaten and jailed (all of which is good on occasion and which we gladly do), the most efficient action and the most significant testimony in favor of nonviolence and truth is living: living a life that is one, where everything goes in the same sense, from prayer and meditation to laboring for our daily bread, from the teaching of the doctrine to the making of manure, from cooking to singing and dancing around the fire; living a life in which there is no violence or unfairness, neither hidden violence nor brutal violence; neither legal and permitted unfairness, nor illegal unfairness. What matters is to show that such a life is possible and even not more difficult than a life of gain, nor more unpleasant than a life of pleasure, nor less natural than an "ordinary" life. What matters is to find the nonviolent answer to all the questions man is faced with today, as at all epochs, to formulate the answer clearly and do our utmost to carry it into effect. What matters is to discover whether there is such a thing as a nonviolent economy, free of all forms of pressure and closed to all forms of unfairness; whether there is such a thing as nonviolent authority, independent of force and carrying no privileges; whether there is such a thing as nonviolent justice, justice without punishment, and punishment without violence; such things as nonviolent farming, nonviolent medicine, nonviolent psychiatry, nonviolent diet.

And to begin with, what matters is to make sure that all violence, even of speech, even of thought, even hidden and disguised, has been weeded out of our religious life.

4

THE ROOT CAUSE
OF WAR

The root cause of war is threefold: possession, power, and justice.

But seeing that possession is a "right" over things, and power is a "right" over men, and that the reasoning animal's whole activity expresses itself in juridical terms, the cause's name can be shortened to *justice.*

The root cause of war and of all wars on both sides: the spirit of justice. "We have the right! We are right! We have been wronged!" There, rightly or wrongly, lies the cause of war.

Justice, or rather the impurity of man's justice; justice combined with covetousness and pride, which are the essence of sin.

The rights claimed being neither of the order of nature nor of the order of the absolute, but fictive and conventional, contestable and contested, the sacred pronouncements can always be juggled with, and this is where the devil enters the game.

Which explains why war is always just, doubly just—just on both sides. And the more just it is, the more atrocities it justifies.

The task of nonviolence is to free man from the chains of legitimate violence and its infernal logic.

5

SEVEN OBVIOUS TRUTHS THAT NOBODY WANTS TO SEE,

or

AXIOMS OF NONVIOLENCE

"Peace" is a strong word. It has the same root as "pact" and presupposes agreement confirmed by sworn faith and the law. It has the same root as "pay" (*pacare* means "to appease") and so implies measured compensation. It is an act, an act that costs an effort. It belongs to the same family as "compact" and implies solidity and coherence.

This simple consideration of the meaning of words reveals the oneness of peace with justice which is stability, balance, and law.

Everyone knows that injustice makes peace impossible, for injustice is a state of violence and disorder which cannot and must not be maintained. It asserts itself through violence, holds sway through violence, and leads to the violence of revolt, which shows that if justice is the reason for peace, it is at the same time the cause of revolution and war, acts that always draw their justification from the defense or conquest of rights and the abolition of injustice.

And this is the crux of the matter: the connection of justice with strife, a truth signified by the sword Justice carries in her right hand. This is no figure of speech. At the heart of all conflict there is the cry, "I am absolutely right! And the brute there, that fiend, will not listen to reason, so that I have not only the right, but the duty to force him, or do away with him."

And there we have the sinews of war and of every quarrel. The causes of war are sometimes attributed to hatred, contempt, pride, envy, covetousness, and other wicked feelings (and sometimes it is true, and sometimes not true at all).

Or they are attributed to our duty to maintain established order, cost what it may. Or to the right and duty to reverse that order at all costs for the sake of the oppressed and exploited and to ensure that the world of tomorrow will be more just.

By which it can be seen that in all human conflict, whether personal or collective, the chain of violence is reinforced by the chain of good reasons, on both sides. It must therefore be admitted that justice is not only the pretext or excuse of violence,. but its very cause. Moreover, whereas one or other of these causes may be absent, justice is always present as a cause and is sometimes the sole cause.

But we started off from justice the foundation of peace, and here we come to justice the cause of all conflict. Are there two justices then?

Yes, the true and the false.

The true, which is one as truth is one. True justice is at one with truth. It is above everything, in everything, inscribed in the order of things, exists by itself and is God.

False justice is double and contradictory and, like mental aberration, engenders illusion and idols. But men cling to these phantoms more tenaciously than to reality, and so are tormented and torn asunder and hurled against each other in the perpetual war named history.

Let no one say of justice what is commonly said of truth:

that it is inaccessible. Say rather that it is inevitable, obvious as light to the eye, and all error claims its support.

How does true justice lapse into false?

By means of these three arguments:

1. *That we have the right to render evil for evil and to call the evil rendered good and just.*

2. *That the end justifies the means and good ends justify bad means.*

3. *That reason, agreement, and consent do not suffice to maintain justice and that it is just to have recourse to fear, compulsion, and force, not only in exceptional cases, but by means of permanent institutions.*

These three arguments are tenets of faith for the common man, for the good as for the wicked. They are never called into doubt, never discussed, and on them people base their civil law and rules of behavior.

It has seldom been noticed that they are self-contradictory and can only lead to endless conflict.

Therefore justice and truth require us to disentangle ourselves from these arguments and their consequences. We must free ourselves from them under penalty of death. For the fact is that if today we cannot find other means of solving human conflict, we are all condemned to die.

The good news that must be announced in our time is that these means have been found. They are the arms of justice, or active revolutionary nonviolence.

The nonviolent can be distinguished by their refusal of the three arguments everyone repeats in order to justify violence. Nonviolence says:

1. *No, evil is not corrected or arrested by an equal evil, but doubled, and to have recourse to it is to become a link in the chain of evil.*

2. *No, the end does not justify the means. Evil means spoil the best causes. If the end is just, the means must be so too.*

3. *No, fear, compulsion, and force can never establish justice, any more than they can teach us truth. They can only twist conscience. Now, the righting of conscience is what is called justice.*

The nonviolent directly adhere to and act from the justice that is one, universal, and as simple as *two-and-two-make-four.* Hunger and thirst for justice are what make them act. They are servants of justice and do not make justice their servant so as to justify acts dictated by the motives mentioned earlier or reactions dictated by the adversary's attitude.

That is why Gandhi names direct nonviolent action "Satyagraha," that is to say, an act of fidelity to truth. The victory the nonviolent seek is to convince the enemy and bring about a change of heart, to convert him by fighting him and, in the end, to make a friend of him.

Is the thing possible? How can it be done? Who has ever done it? In what circumstances, and with what results? I shall not answer here. Whole books have been written on the subject.

The first thing is to learn and understand what it is; the second, to try it out for oneself. But it cannot be learned like arithmetic or grammar. Learning and understanding nonviolence are done from within. So the first steps are self-recollection, reflection on the principles, and conversion, that is to say, turning back against the common current.

For if the purpose of your action is to make the adversary change his mind without forcing him to, how can you do so unless you yourself are converted? If the purpose is to wrest the enemy from his hatred and his evil by touching his conscience, how can you do so if you have not freed yourself from hatred, evil, and lack of conscience? You want to bring peace into the world, which is very generous of you; peace to the uttermost ends of the earth, for you are great-hearted, but do you know how to bring peace into your own house? Is there peace in your heart? Can one give what one does not possess?

As for justice, can you establish it between yourself and others, even those who are strangers and hostile to you, if you cannot succeed with your nearest and dearest? And what is more, if you cannot establish it between you and yourself?

But do not jump to the discouraging conclusion that in order to enter nonviolent combat one must be a saint or a wise man, or perfect. This form of combat is for one and all, and we can enter it as we are, with our indignities (and even all the better as we are fully conscious of them). But we should know that in principle, if not in fact, we must prepare ourselves as for all struggle. Here, however, preparation must be inward.

On the other hand, the struggle itself and the tribulations it involves are exercises that will help our transformation, and self-mastery is a pledge of victory over evil.

Peace and justice are a harmonious adjustment which does not come about by itself but is the fruit of effort and work upon oneself, before and during confrontation. That is why Vinoba says, "The training ground for nonviolence is man's heart."

But drill is not enough, nor courage, nor reason. There must also be music and a sense of harmony.

Let us proceed to the other tenets of everyman's faith:

4. *All violence, including murder, becomes lawful in the case of self-defense.* Another argument that no one calls in doubt. Do you? Yes. Because self-defense is legitimate, a right and a duty, but murder, which is offense, not defense, is not.

Therefore one should not speak of legitimate defense, but of justified offense, which is self-contradictory.

I have no more right to take someone's life in order to defend mine than I have to take his wife in order to ensure my own happiness.

Let it rather be called "natural" or "animal" defense. It is of capital importance not to drag the law into this matter.

For if we consider legitimate the exceptional case where one can see no other means of staving off aggression than killing, we shall build up on it a whole system of legislation and institutions whose sole office will be to prepare and perpetuate murder.

And that is what we have done. The army, the police, and criminal law are that and nothing else.

Defense will no longer be natural and for that reason excusable; it will be premeditated and systematic crime, and there will no longer be any moral restraint or limit to killing and cruelty.

5. *Murder is not only permissible, but a duty when common welfare requires it.* Now the "common welfare" in question is not the welfare of all. It is the welfare of a limited group, even if it includes millions of people (the number involved makes no difference). Common welfare cannot be achieved at anyone's expense. Common welfare is justice and charity toward every human being.

6. *Technology, economy, and politics are morally neutral. They obey their own natural laws.* Here is how men build the gigantic machinery in which they are caught and crushed.

That efficiency is good and always necessary for doing something goes without saying, but it is senseless to attribute value to it in itself. If efficiency lies in doing evil, then the better it is, the worse it is.

7. *Justice is established order.* This seventh argument, unlike those that have gone before, is not accepted by everyone. There is no regime which does not have its rebels. But the conviction of the greater number is such that the ordinary citizen is ready to kill and die through obedience to law and power.

Now the law fixes morals. Morals are the effect of a certain balance of force between tribes and classes, hard-won pacts which make possible civil life and work in common.

By the standards of absolute justice, the law always has lamentable shortcomings, in addition to which holders of power commit errors and abuses, all of which is coated over by habit and ignorance. But should the balance of power shift, consciences awake, and there ensues revolt which results in the creation of other states of injustice.

There must therefore always be a law to correct the law, and the law is constantly having to be amended and adjusted, as in liberal regimes.

But liberal regimes are unstable and continually shaken by rivalry, so that governments have more to do to stay in power than to govern. Nevertheless, they still have enough strength to abuse their power, and the people enough passion and blindness to abuse their right of opposition. The liberal regime is no doubt more humane than others, but criticism by the opposition is less pure because it requires less courage. Legal and licit means exist of denouncing injustice in the press and raising questions in parliament, but the rich, the powerful, and the intriguers remain masters of the game.

That is why one must have no fear of resorting to direct nonviolent action and, if necessary, of breaking the law openly, seeking legal punishment and undertaking fasts and other sacrifices, so that the justice which is above all law may dawn in men's consciences.

This does not mean that direct nonviolent action is impossible in nonliberal regimes. To be sure, it is more difficult, and victory less certain.

But whoever does not attempt it at a relatively easy stage deserves to fall into bondage and undergo dictatorship.

Murderous rebellion, disorder, and cowardly acquiescence alike foster tyrannical regimes.

PART TWO

TACTICS OF
NONVIOLENCE:
THE CAMPAIGNS

I

AGAINST TORTURE

AN APPEAL TO CONSCIENCE AND A FAST
March 1957

An Appeal to the Conscience of the French Nation

France is still loved in the world as one of the freest and most humane of nations.

If we are not free to cry out against the horror that fills us, if our cry does not startle the French conscience, then France is no more.

Water is poured into a funnel, the funnel is stuck into a man's throat. The man's stomach swells until it bursts.

Buried alive, all but the head.

The electric rod. Salt rubbed into wounds.

Electric current switched onto the sexual organs or the ear.

Teeth, nails, eyes torn out.

These are a few of the methods of pacification in Algeria.

The suspect are subjected to them. The suspect, those who are suspected of knowing something. If they do not speak because they know nothing, or because they are too proud to sell their comrades, the torture is prolonged, until death if need be.

Oradour is multiplied. Tanks crush houses, sometimes also the people inside them, including mothers and children.

Ask those who come back. Ask them yourself. Not all speak, not all are willing to, but there is no one who does not know. Fifteen years afterward, we are now beginning to inflict on others the atrocities the Gestapo inflicted on us.

For their war crimes, their commanding officers were sentenced to be hanged, those who carried out their orders, to be shot. They roused our indignation and that of the whole world.

"But," people will say, "our enemies also torture and mutilate." We know. We know all the better as one of our own Companions was murdered. We grieve for him. But we answer without hesitation, *Other people's wrongs do not make us right.*

We do not approve of their crimes any more than we approve of our own, but we repeat, *Other people's wrongs do not make us right.*

Besides, atrocity does not put an end to atrocity, but causes and redoubles it.

You who love France and want to save her from shame and downfall must dare to denounce this abomination. Write to your members of parliament, ministers, and prefects [provincial representatives of the government], and demand that, on our side at least, it be stopped at once.

People will say that to broadcast such things is to soil our flag and dishonor our country. To which we answer, *What soils and dishonors it is to do these things, not to tell of them; and now, whoever remains silent becomes an accomplice of the crime.*

But who are we? And what are we aiming at? On whose side are we playing? Who has encouraged us? Who is paying us?

We are men free of all ties, obeying our own hearts.

We are men from whom these horrors have taken the taste for bread.

We accuse no one; we feel deeply that the faults committed in our name are our fault.

For our fault, for our enemies' fault, we shall abstain from all food for twenty days, taking water only, until Easter, and we shall stay in Paris exposed to the public view for all that time.

This is a dumb cry, a dumb prayer, a living sacrifice.

We implore every passerby, every Christian, every decent person in France to reflect, to come to his senses, and then to act according to his conscience.

LANZA DEL VASTO
BERNARD GASCHARD, farmer
PIERRE PARODI, doctor

On the other side of the same tract:

An Appeal to the Heads of Islam and to the Leaders of the "National Liberation Front" of Algeria

You are not unaware that there are Christians in France demanding justice for Algeria. I am one of them. I am also a disciple of Gandhi, Gandhi who was always a friend to Islam. It was because he had brought about peace with Pakistan that he died a martyr.

The cruelty, the torture, the collective reprisals, the crimes which my fellow countrymen have added to the wretchedness of war, fill me with horror and shame.

In consequence, I find myself compelled by the spirit to fast, with two of my Companions, for twenty days and nights in a place open to the public, imploring God to forgive us, entreating the people of France to protest against these abominations and demand that they be stopped. The fact is that most of our people do not know of these things or cannot believe that they exist; I do not doubt that, as soon as they know, every Christian, every decent person will cry out against them as I am doing.

You know, on the other hand, that your people, too, frequently torture and mutilate and kill innocent persons, women and children, which is as contrary to your law as it is to ours.

Do not think I am proposing a pact or a bargain. I am not saying, "If your people stop, ours will too." Do not say to me, "When yours have stopped, we shall urge ours to stop too."

The first to stop will be able to raise his eyes toward heaven again.

May God put peace into us and between us.

Lanza del Vasto
March 31, 1957

To Our Friends

Our cause is in the hands of God. We have only to suffer and wait. We have chosen the better part. Why should we be anxious? They can do nothing to us. If they let us be, it is scandalous; if they arrest us, it is more scandalous still. As Abbé Pierre says, "They are lions and we are a flea. That is why we are stronger than they, for a flea can bite a lion but a lion can't bite a flea." We shall be the flea that bites conscience.

That several hearts be touched, that a fold of the sordid curtain of indifference be raised for a moment, that a few wretched victims be snatched from the hands of their torturers, that a step be taken toward appeasement, that the "force of truth" reveal once more what it can do—is what we are asking of God.

I warn you earnestly against the common argument that the enemy also commits atrocities, and more of them. I answer this argument in my two appeals, but it is one that has to be countered at every turn, for it is tenacious. The itch to judge is constant.

More or *less* has nothing to do with it. One crime is enough to make a criminal, one theft to make a thief. One Oradour is enough to turn a regiment into a band of Nazis.

Now, if we are to believe one of the few Moslem appeals that has managed to reach us, we have to account for the devastation of whole regions, the massacre of six hundred thousand women, children, and old people, the destruction of villages with phosphorus bombs and napalm.[1] We cannot check these figures, nobody can at the moment. We hope they are hundreds of times, six hundred thousand times overestimated!

Whatever our friends do, we beg them, at least for the moment, to forget their opinions and political passions. There is no room for them here, for, if they advance them, the cohesion that might take place between all who want to participate in Satyagraha will be broken, whereas each one of us, whether he be white, red, or gray, has the same lump in his throat when he hears of atrocities; it is enough to be a man. All of us can ask God to forgive our brothers who, of their own will or under duress, are carrying out this vile, atrocious task. And we can shout to them to stop.

Is *that* an opinion?

Opinions we may have like everybody else. We may have our own answers to the question of the legitimacy of war in general and of this one in particular. We may have our own opinion as to whether it is right, or not, to possess colonies;

whether Algeria is a French province;

whether it is appropriate to call what we are doing there "pacification" and to treat the enemy like a band of criminals;

whether the Algerian nation exists;

whether we should treat with them or wait for a second Dien

---

[1] *An Appeal from the People of Algeria*, published in *L'Essor* (Geneva, March 1957). It goes without saying that the French press is perfectly free to speak of the crimes of the terrorists, but when it denounces those of the police and the army, it does so at its own risk.

Bien Phu or a new atomic threat from Russia or renewed remonstrances from America or another condemnation by the United Nations,

or else simply drown the uprising in blood.

Concerning all these questions, which it is customary to call "complex," we are ready to believe that we are not fully informed and that in any case, we have neither the duty nor the competence to lay down the law. But we hope to have enough courage to keep our useless opinions to ourselves.

But supposing that at some time during these twenty days we received news of a truce, would we break off our penance?

No.

And if there were a cease-fire?

No.

For we are not fasting *in order to obtain something*, even such a desirable thing as peace. We are fasting to expiate.

The most we could do would be to give up fasting in public and come down from our pillory to hide at home.

Several of our dearest friends have taken alarm at the length of our fast, not wishing to see us suffer, and fearing for our lives. Some have even tried to strike an affectionate bargain and get us to reduce our sentence to a fortnight. Others are afraid that this excessive ordeal may appear to be a feat of strength, a sort of fakir's exhibition. We are fully aware of these dangers, and of the second above all. But we have been inwardly prompted to do this thing in this measure.

And when we compare the measure with the tide of evil we are trying to stem, it seems small indeed.

For even if it were to sweep our lives away, the measure would still be too small.

But from the fact that our suffering, during these last days of Lent, joins that of Christ, we dare to hope that some share of His infinite merit may give our sacrifice its worth.

THE TWENTY DAYS

The ultra-jingoistic newspaper which published the series of events that roused public opinion and prepared or accompanied our Satyagraha like a "cunningly orchestrated newspaper campaign," "a plot," a series of *coups de théâtre* staged by politics and finance, at least had on its side the support of likelihood in that there is sense and order in the facts presented.

Here is a short summary of these events, unforeseen when, at the beginning of March, we took the decision to fast.

Toward the twelfth of March, Pierre-Henri Simon's book *Against Torture* came out, and a few days later, *Le Monde*, a moderate and objective newspaper, published an article on the front page. Whereupon, in a prison in Algiers, the suicide of a barrister named Ali Boumendjel took place. Having been illegally imprisoned by the parachutists, he had been "questioned" by them for over a month, after their fashion.

This was immediately followed by a protest from René Capitant, who suspended his lecture in the Faculty of Law in Paris.

Meanwhile, *L'Express* published Servan-Schreiber's account, "A Lieutenant in Algeria," and the Minister of National Defense announced punishments for people who disparaged the army by speaking of atrocities, and immediately attacked *L'Express* for publishing a photograph which was not an authentic document. (What should have been proved was that the text was not trustworthy evidence.) Now, in the text, there were such statements as these: "in some districts, one dowar out of two is laid waste"; "the army is rotting from the head downward and generals are made by politics"; "in some places the army is an active element of counter-terrorism"; "the rebels take three times more arms from the French Army than they have been able to receive from outside"; "whether fresh to the army or having done long service, the military are being turned into racist murderers, good-for-nothings and sometimes even fiends."

These are the things which the ministry should clearly prove to be false, instead of attacking a photograph.

Next appeared the statement of a "Commission of Inquiry" which sat in Oran for fifty days, questioning prisoners on the treatment they had undergone. (These prisoners were all French, it seems, and exposed to the revenge of those they might denounce.) The investigators conclude that it is impossible to prove that the persons they have been allowed to see have been tortured, but their statement is muddled and ends with a vindication of "exceptional measures" (in other words, illegal arrest and the extortion of confession by any means whatever). In addition to this, one member of the commission has refused to sign. From all this, common sense draws proof of what was not to be proved.

Then came the statement of the cardinals and archbishops, containing clear references to the atrocities. (It was we and our friends who supplied the Assembly with the documents by which we ourselves had been convinced. We also presented them to the President of the Republic.)

At a meeting on the twelfth of March, the Protestant Federation had also taken a stand; it denounced the facts with greater precision: "The evidence received comes from too many sources and is of too reliable a quality, the ill-treatment too serious and too well vouched for, the feelings of many soldiers and officers too painful for us not to appeal to public conscience . . ." "We are convinced that defending honor consists in stamping out evil practices, not in blaming those who denounce them."

Témoignage Chrétien, L'Express, France-Observateur, and *Le Monde* now spoke openly of torture and atrocity. Thirty thousand copies of *Evidence from Servicemen* were printed. This pamphlet was published by our Committee of Spiritual Resistance and endorsed by about sixty signatures covering the witnesses whom we are protecting from possible reprisals. The document is appalling and irrefutable. Rescued from seizure by the police, it was sent to everyone holding office, and widely distributed in Paris and the provinces. The public seized upon it.

Socialist students protested, the universities protested. The Minister of Justice himself asked for explanations. The Radical Party asked the Minister of Defense to make a statement. He defended himself in the usual manner, attacking the accusers and covering the torturers. He had the effrontery to claim that the witnesses were all blameworthy, not because they had denounced the crimes, but because they had not denounced them in time, that is to say, to their commanding officers when they were in service, for of course the high command knew nothing about them, reproved them, and—when it found out about them—punished them.

But, unluckily for the Minister of Defense, this assertion was publicly and forcefully refuted by General Paris de Bollardière, a hero of the Resistance who asked to be relieved of his command, showing thereby that the barbaric orders came from above him. He also wrote to Servan-Schreiber to congratulate him on his report and confirm the truth of it. (It is Bollardière's own struggle with conscience that Servan-Schreiber describes as that of "Colonel Galland.") For this act of indiscipline, Bollardière was confined to a fortress for two months. Shantidas wrote to him: "All the glory and decorations won on so many battlefields are not worth as much, in our eyes, as your courage in refusing to obey inane and impious orders."

When so many persons of feeling, Catholics and Protestants,

men of law and military, journalists and religious rise up together without having given each other the word, then the hand
of God must be in it. Convinced of this, we entered the lists
too. To be sure, there have been other scandals since the Ark
came into existence. "Why have you suddenly gone into action?"
some asked. The answer is, "Because we were waiting for a
sign and now have one."

Till the very last minute, we could not decide upon the place
of sacrifice. At first, we had thought of some old boat, some
tarred landing-stage moored to a quay of the Seine. We were
not daunted by the picturesqueness of such an abode or the
probable jibes and jeering songs of onlookers. It would be a very
pleasant pillory. But it would have been on the route planned
for the Queen of England whose visit we were expecting. To
put a blot of penance in the midst of the celebrations would
have been ungallant, and a celebration of friendship between
two peoples is not the sort of feast at which we like to play the
skeleton. We thought of the cloister in the Church of St.
Séverin, whose iron grillwork would separate us from the street
without shielding us from view and whose arches would
shelter us from rain and the night. But we were afraid of
bringing trouble to that friendly parish, situated in a tumultuous
quarter. We could still have asked Abbé Pierre for shelter,
since we were homeless. But Abbé Pierre was busy in Morocco
with the biggest undertaking of his life. Shantidas did not see
him till the night before the fast, and seeing him so tired and
burdened with other cares, was glad not to have to ask him for
anything. He preferred to listen to him talking on his favorite
subject: "Let whoever suffers most be served first," also, about
a commentary on "Our Father who art in heaven" which he was
going to have to recite into some broadcasting machine, "but
it's a good exercise and a real rest to talk about it to a live
human being, face to face."

On the morning of the first of April, the three fasters went and took up their post at Clichy. From their neighbors, three Africans, they learned straight away that it was the first day of Ramadan. They took this for a sign.

14, rue de Landy. We had not chosen the place, but had been invited two days previously by someone who lived there. We only knew that it was a very poor house, and that had decided us. And we soon perceived that there were reasons for choosing this place in preference to all others, and there again we saw signs.

In the age of Louis XIV, Clichy was a village and St. Vincent de Paul was its vicar. Just a few steps from our lodging, in the yard near the church, you can still see the tree under which the Father of the Poor would sit and read his breviary.

In this sordid quarter, where no likeness of what once was survives, where a multitude of small factories drone and grate upon the ear, where trucks maneuver, feathers of soot rain down, smutting windows and blackening façades, where gaunt, lopsided buildings patched with posters rear up with ludicrous gestures, the presence of the saint can still be felt, and traces of him live on.

Opposite, Jeunesse Ouvrière Catholique (Young Catholic Workers' Movement) came into being.

Beside it, the charitable association of the Boy Singers of the Wooden Cross.

Farther down the street, Le Nid (The Nest), a home for girls taken off the streets.

On the other side of the church, the headquarters of International Civil Service.

There is also a team of young men who have dedicated themselves to the conversion of drunkards, pimps, and homosexuals.

A dangerous apostolate, full of preposterous adventures. They have already saved three thousand drinkers and consequently three thousand families. To keep the man they have rescued on his new path, they make him a colleague and he helps to rescue others.

The small house we are in is a hostel for homeless young workingmen, and the founder, himself a young workman, is our friend and host. Thirty-two people in addition to his family live within its crumbling walls. Among them, former drunkards and their families, some Moroccans and a Negro.

That very evening, there is a friendly get-together of the whole neighborhood with people introducing themselves, and a talk.

"Behind a small single-story, leprous, creeping house, through a half-opened door, you see a yard, poor but not dirty—flowers on the windowsills, a noise of children, washing blowing in the wind. On the right, in a big, open shed, a ring of benches and rickety chairs around a fire that sends up a gentle smoke from between three paving-stones" (*Combat*, April 17).

There our twenty days went by without our feeling weak or giddy. We had no mishaps or excessive pain. Right to the end, we were able to get up and take a cold shower, wash our linen, answer news reporters, meet our friends, take part in discussions, and give lectures.

In the evening, we stirred the fire into flame, and standing around it with French and African workmen of the neighborhood, as well as our companions and friends, we said our open prayer together and exchanged the kiss of peace.

During the first week, the newspapers granted these occurrences only a brief line or two. Toward the end of the second week (April 12), an article appeared in *Témoignage Chrétien*. Fasting was considered in its biblical, Christian, and Gandhian context, and there were quotations from Abbé Pierre, who had mentioned us in the leader of his review *"Faim et Soif"* (Hunger and Thirst) and in his public talks. The article, interesting in itself, had the additional interest of being signed by Maurice Vaussard, president of Pax Christi, closely associated with the Archbishopric. Then, in *Combat* (April 17), an article appeared with the title "Gandhi Alive" and further articles appeared in *Libération* (April 17) and *L'Express* (April 19).[2]

No French newspaper dared to publish the whole of the two appeals, and no French or French-speaking radio mentioned them. However, they appeared in Morocco (*Al Istiqlal*, April 13) and were broadcast in Arabic and French by the Moroccan radio. And so they reached the Moslems to whom they were addressed.

On the whole, the press was remarkably discreet and favorable. There were not many insults or jokes. What was to be feared—that loud, crude publicity would misrepresent our action, spoil its effect, and make it ridiculous—was avoided by the silence of the newspapermen, which should be seen as a form of respect. To tell the truth, fasting was then such a novelty in the West that nobody knew what to say or think of it. "The presence of a strange force," whispered some.

A friend of ours had accused us of "going in for politics now" or, at least, "playing into the hands of certain parties." But no politician and no party made the mistake of thinking so. "Lanza del Vasto, without being an enemy to the Communists (nor to anybody else), turns his back directly on them," observed Hélène Tuzet. The extreme left-wing *Mouvement de la Paix* demonstrated on the twelfth against the torture going on, but there was no confusion, collusion, or meeting with us, nor any mention in their press of our gesture. In any case, it seems im-

[2] See this article in the Appendix.

possible that the Ark should be confused with or even enter into agreement with any party, movement, or group whatever, even when it occasionally makes common cause with one. People do not come to the Ark in a body, they do not come because they belong to such and such a class or nation or profession or school, but often, on the contrary, because they are in conflict with their group. Even the Committee of Spiritual Resistance, of which Shantidas is a member and Roland Marin, our Companion, the secretary, limited its "resistance" to the publication of *Evidence from Servicemen* and declined responsibility for the fast in which the Ark alone was involved.

And here is how, willy-nilly, for better or for worse I can't tell, we were reduced to our own resources. Our aim was to appeal to the greatest possible number of people, so we had 150,000 copies of the tract printed and set about distributing it with the help of our Companions, friends, and groups.

Girls and boys formed teams to help us. Faithful friends came from the provinces to join them, as well as young people from the hostel, and willing passers-by. People in offices received the leaflet by mail. It was handed out on the boulevards, in the subway, at factory gates, in church porches. There was some obstruction and rough handling. The police picked up our boys all over town, but as soon as they had been released, they started again.

A number of Christians, touched by our message, greeted, supported, or rallied to us. I say Christians, for Catholics and Protestants upheld us in the same measure, in prayer and in deed. *There* is the true unity of the churches, without artifice or ulterior motives, without controversy or compromise, without precaution or effort. Even if we had obtained no other result than this (in such close accordance with the vocation of the Ark), it would have been worthwhile. It began with the visit of the four curates and the kind vicar of our parish (Monsieur Vincent's successor). After that, they brought new friends to us several times a day and asked their parishioners to join us in our fast, at least on Good Friday. St. Sulpice and various churches in Paris, Lyons, and Dijon did likewise. *The Parish Newssheet of the Loop of the Seine* boldy printed our appeal and so did *Cité Nouvelle* (The New City), a Protestant review. Pastor Trocmé came and fasted with us for a day. Fathers Journet and Régamey paid us several visits. Louis Massignon also came several times and prayed in our rooms, and toward the end Abbé Pierre came and embraced us.

Every morning, bundles of letters arrived from friends, famous persons, and above all, unknown people—soldiers whose hearts our appeal had touched, for they had, with their own eyes, witnessed some of the atrocities we were denouncing. One soldier who had been released from service affirmed that he had seen no such thing during all the months of his campaign, but contrary to the government's declaration, his was an isolated and very exceptional case. Schoolchildren wrote to us promising not to eat chocolate during the whole of Lent. We also received letters of abuse, at least three with each mail. (How is it that those who insult us all have the same arguments, the same style, and the same handwriting?)

As for the Algerian leaders, we found out from a priest who was in touch with them that our appeal had been received and heard. They had immediately grasped its sacred character. Furthermore, the life of the Companions of the Ark, outside business, intrigue, and ambition, added "to their gesture the weight of truth." It is quite remarkable that Moslems today have no hope or confidence except in Christians. This is thanks to the courageous representations of the Bishop of Algiers and the firm moderation of priests who are now in jail, of Foucauld's *"petits frères"* and white monks who have stayed in the hills and dowars while the war rages around them. It is also due to the present movement of opinion in the capital, which is above all an awakening of Christian conscience. We have received no direct response, however, and no Algerian has come to fast with us in expiation of his crimes and ours, as we had hoped.[3]

The nights have passed well, with light sleep or serene sleeplessness. I think of M. Guy Mollet, M. Bourgès-Maunoury, and M. Lacoste, and of us three on our planks. Oh, the poor fellows! How much better to be in our place than in theirs.

In the morning I look at the five beautiful tulips a neighbor has brought us. Cut off from their roots as we are, they have been living for a fortnight on love and fresh water. Dawn descends from the skylight and springs up again in their fresh flame, and my prayer and my meditation consist in losing my sight in their live color. The lesson they teach me is that life is good in itself and not happy because of pleasure; that it is pure joy, beyond pleasure and pain, perfect joy because it is a gift of God, God's gift of Himself, since He says, "I am Life." Objects of desire must be seen through, one must look through them without dwelling on them or leaving one's heart in them, or letting parts of oneself cling to them. The source of desire must become the only object of desire; then the circle is closed, for the source of desire is the life we have in us. The pleasure we think we derive from things is a veil that hides life from us; push the veil aside and you will discover that life is all joy. Likewise, pain is a veil that hides death from us, push it aside and you will discover that death is deliverance and place. Fasting teaches me this certainty and makes me touch it. We fear death not because it is painful but because we fear it will become painful. We fear it because we cling to the husk we take for ourselves but which is our cage; we cling to the body believing it our support, whereas it is the weight that

---

[3] The Communists, who have espoused the cause of the Moslems, repel them by their materialist theories and their rejection of tradition. Besides, the Algerian patriots find it hard to understand how anyone can take up arms against his own country, even to come to their aid.

drags us down, for we believe that the little life it contains is the only life and defend it desperately against death, which we see as black nothingness. But death is the infinite—seizing us in its blaze, the tide of infinite life taking us up. Whoever fasts sees death rising from hour to hour without fear, without regret, without tragic feeling, without funereal thoughts, without ghosts. He is astonished not to encounter the suffering he has been going toward wholeheartedly.

On the last day, a telegram arrived from India:

GOD BLESS YOUR SATYAGRAHA. I HOPE TO HELP IN MELTING MY HEART WITH LOVE.

VINOBA

2

AGAINST
THE BOMB

THE ATTACK ON MARCOULE
April 1958

The first camp opened at Sénos by the Companions of the Ark for the study of nonviolence had a happy outcome in that it ended by a campaign, and a campaign is better than a camp.

As you know, it was not limited to Friends of the Ark: all kinds of associations were invited and came: two priests, a Dominican, Father Journet, Pastor Trocmé of the International Movement of Reconciliation, Robert Barrat, Alfred Nahon, members of the International Civil Service, of Foucauld's Fraternité Séculière, Camille Drevet of the Friends of Gandhi Association, Olga Birioukoff, the daughter of Tolstoy's late secretary, conscientious objectors, Quakers, and Emmaus volunteers. There were fine talks and moving reports. But the most applauded speech was no doubt the briefest, that of Shantidas proposing to put an end to the talking and to break into the neighboring plant at Marcoule, where, in spite of official denials, everybody knows that the first French atomic bomb was being prepared.

Everybody also knows that if France has its bomb, another ten nations will soon have theirs.

The explanation with which we are hoodwinked is that the

Bomb is being manufactured in order not to use it, for that would be too terrible and too crazy, but everybody knows that it was already used during the last war, and that nothing is too terrible or too crazy for those who make war. The Bomb, they say, is for frightening the enemy, who will not ask for more. But the enemy will be frightened only if he thinks we are going to use it. We cannot at the same time frighten him and re-assure ourselves. Fear can only incite the enemy to make his own bomb and throw it at us first. Everybody knows that it is fear (much more than hatred or any other reason) that makes war break out.

But there is no need for an outbreak of war for the Bomb to be fearsome. Einstein, Schweitzer, Oppenheimer, Joliot-Curie, and hundreds of other scientists have proved and proclaimed that tests will suffice to obscure the sun, disintegrate the earth, attack the organs and the seed of man and animals, strike some with impotency and sterility, condemn others to engender monsters, and that they whiten the blood and rot the flesh with hidden leprosy. Air, water, food, the sea, rain, and wind can all become carriers of death for the whole of mankind.

But for a small wage, people continue calmly to manufacture their own death.

Sometimes I shout to them, "Can it be possible that you have so little imagination? Do you really have to be killed in order to understand what you are doing?"

In America, our *Catholic Worker* friends have repeatedly fasted, made public protests, and published appeals ever since the crime of Hiroshima. Their latest undertaking was to get themselves jailed for attempting to break through the security cordon during the experiments in Nevada.

Other war-resisters refused to take shelter during compulsory air-raid exercises.

Four Americans (black, it seems) are going to England, France, Germany, and Russia in order to approach the governments of these countries and rouse public concern.

On the fourth of April, the writer William Bross Lloyd, Dr. Linus Pauling, Nobel Prize winner for chemistry, the socialist Norman Thomas, and other American citizens brought a lawsuit against Mr. Neil H. McElroy, Secretary of Defense, Mr. Lewis L. Strauss, President of the Atomic Energy Commission, and several of its members.

The plaintiffs want the law to compel the accused to abstain from further atomic armament experiments until they have furnished proof in court that these experiments are not contrary to constitutional guarantees and American law.

In Switzerland, for several years now, Alfred Nahon has been expressing his alarm by appeals to public opinion and fasts of as long as nineteen days. He wants to start a chain of short but continual fasts.

But the most heroic and the most moving Satyagraha was that undertaken by the Quaker Albert Smith-Bigelow and three companions, all middle-aged men with families. They rigged a ship, the *Golden Rule*, and having set sail from Honolulu on the twenty-fourth of April, headed in spite of the warnings of the authorities for the forbidden zone where a bomb was to be launched, fifty times more destructive than that of Hiroshima and "almost clean," as the experts announced with a simper. To the harbormaster who said to him, "You are going to certain death," the captain of the *Golden Rule* replied, "We want to say to all men, be honest with yourselves."

In England, a radioactive accident which spoiled the milk of a whole district, and which it was impossible to conceal, brought some people to their senses, and although such and such a bishop declared that the manufacture of the Bomb was in conformity with the gospel, and such and such a head of state that it was in conformity with prudence and necessary for the good of all, they have not convinced everyone.

During the Easter holidays, a dramatic event took place. Four thousand persons went on foot to Aldermaston where the H-bomb is being manufactured and stood massed before the gates where they were cheered by the population and harassed by hostile propaganda with howling slogans from publicity vans and planes. A press campaign attempted in vain to cast ridicule on the demonstration, which, on the contrary, was remarkable for its dignified and even religious attitude. Moreover, it had been prepared and inspired by the eighty-year-old philosopher Bertrand Russell, Commander King-Hall, Canon Collins, and other personalities famous for their scientific, political, and even military past.

And the sensation caused by the resignation, last year, of eighteen West German scientists has not been forgotten.

Our expedition was improvised; no sooner had the proposal been made than it was adopted without discussion and carried out next day.

Out of the 120 persons who were attending the "Information Camp," 82 took part wholeheartedly in the adventure, spontaneously putting nonviolent discipline into practice.

We had thought of leaving our Companion Denise at home, for she was eight months pregnant. She restrained her tears, but when the moment came to leave, Nicodème, her husband, came to Shantidas with trembling lips and said that if Companions were not to be allowed to bear testimony under the pretext that children are born to them, it would have been as well to prevent them from marrying. He got his way. Souricette (Little Mouse), who is twelve, was also in the party and behaved bravely indeed when her time came.

On Friday, the eleventh of April, toward four o'clock in the afternoon, on a bright, chilly day with the mistral blowing, our little band entered the forbidden territory.

Surrounded like a concentration camp by wire netting, the monstrous, freshly painted factory looked like a seaside holiday building encircled by the sunny hills of the condemned countryside.

Our orders were as follows: to go up to the glass-paned guardhouse, like a group of sightseers who have lost their way. Then, while our three spokesmen are talking with the guards and keeping them as busy as possible, suddenly stoop and go under the barrier (like those at level crossings).

Then go along the road as fast as possible, without running, turning our heads, or answering anybody, and without a shout or a word.

Stick closely round our leaders in tight rows, and shield them from the security men so as to leave them an open passage.

If hit, don't fight back; if somebody else gets hit or falls, don't stop and help; if captured, don't struggle, but, as soon as the guard tries to drag you, sit down and don't move. But if he lets you go in order to seize somebody else, get up and join the others.

If the guards take aim and threaten to shoot, stand still and wait for the leaders' orders.

Keep yourself relaxed and collected, attentive and open.

Our best weapon was the surprise that dumbfounded the guards. When they came to, we were already well ahead. We were therefore free to cover the two hundred yards or so that lay between us and the offices we intended to invade, and we did so as if we had wings, but finding the doors shut, we formed a group in front of the windows. Other guards surrounded us. There were about a score of them, with revolvers in their belts.

To the engineer who had been dispatched to parley with us,

we declared that we were there to protest and would leave only if forced to. We asked to see the chief and handed over a letter for him. As the chief was absent, we asked to see the deputy in command. But the deputy, a military man, refused to see us under these conditions. However, he shortly afterward came down. There was a crossfire of questions and answers.

At first, the tone was haughty. "I can't allow this sort of thing, sir . . . It's beyond me how people can behave like this. You call yourselves nonviolent and you trespass on private property, putting yourselves in the wrong to start with."

"Private? Not at all! On private property what people do is their own business, but what you are doing at Marcoule concerns the whole of France and is everybody's business."

"But supposing I came to your kitchen and refused to get out?" asked the most indignant of them.

"We would give you some soup."

And the most indignant of them smiled.

Another came on the scene with fresh supplies of anger.

"Are you aware that you are acting in a completely illegal manner and that we are entitled to have you forcibly ejected?"

"Yes, we know."

"Well, then?"

"Go ahead, do it."

Others came to reason with us—and show how utterly useless it was to act as we were doing.

Time passed; the cold was piercing. We sat down on the ground and huddled together.

"Do you want to stay here all night? Do you want to stay for three days? Do so by all means. But you will be the first to get tired. You're beaten beforehand without our lifting a finger."

It is a great pity that this was merely an idle threat. There could not have been better conditions for Satyagraha.

Night was falling, and we were becoming chilled. We started

to sing "Alle Psallite," clapping our hands to keep time. Then silence fell.

"Well, what do you want us to do to you?" exclaimed the head guard. Pastor Trocmé spoke.

"Have you a son?"

"Yes."

"What age is he?"

"Five."

"Do to us what you would do to him."

"Look here," said the man with his common sense and strong southern accent, "can you see me smacking your bottoms? I'd look silly, and so would you."

One of us, taking up the attack, took his turn at asking a question.

"Isn't the Bomb a matter of conscience?"

The engineers took refuge behind the usual arguments, but an ordinary sort of fellow, some kind of cleaner or odd-job man, was heard to mutter grimly, "A matter of conscience? Indeed it is!"

"Do you think we want the Bomb any more than you do?" shouted an employee.

"Act like us, then; refuse to make it!"

An inspector came up to us with a worried look.

"Listen, as man to man, won't you explain? I'm trying to understand."

I feel that if they *had* left us there three days, we should not have wasted our time.

But at that point three brigades of state police from Nîmes came into action. Their chief came up and ordered us to clear off, and when we refused to do so, he promised to "make things hot for us."

But the threat was slow in coming and the difficult warming-up process did not last.

The first group to lay hands on Companions and drag them

by the shoulders or the feet surrounded themselves with a fog of filthy words in order to gain courage. They kicked and slapped the men they were dragging, grabbed them by their hair or beards. One of us had his shoulder dislocated, another, his cassock torn, but as they got on with the job, their roughness began to diminish.

When my turn came, I observed more clearly what had become apparent to me as soon as the game had begun. I was an actor in a role written beforehand, a spectator amused by the play being enacted and curious to see what would follow, and I was he who "only stands and waits" in prayer during the fight, repeating, "May Thy servants serve Thee and Thy Will be done."

People said to us, "What's the use of it all?"

They are right. It's of no use at all if we remain alone.

That is why the Companions are now going from door to door to try and rouse the neighborhood and summon people to resist.

We must not say it, lest we discourage those who want to follow us, but it is true: it's of no use.

At least, it's of no use in preventing the Bomb.

The Bomb will go off because we more than deserve it.

It will go off because we shall reap as we have sown.

It will go off, and nothing can prevent it, because the evil has been done.

The worst evil is to have invented it. The supreme sin, the worst sacrilege is to have split the atom. Nothing is more opposed to the creative act of God.

The antithesis of all wisdom, of all kindness, of all spiritual or natural life. God said, "Because thou hast done this, thou shalt surely die." God is not condemning with anger, but observing with sadness that the thief of the fruit of knowledge has condemned himself to death.

To escape his fate, it is not just the Bomb he must give up, but the whole system of which the Bomb is the necessary fruit, being its most perfect expression.

But who submits to the evidence?

Whoever builds the Ark. Everybody else collaborates in the manufacture of the Bomb.

Do you think we want the Bomb? say its makers.

It is not enough not to want it. You must want not to make it. You must want not to let it be made.

You must want not to profit by all the things that go to make it.

You must understand that if we do not give up these things, they will be taken from us all the same, for it is our obstinate clinging to them that will destroy them.

But the Bomb will have to explode because nobody wants to understand.

So people are right to say to us, "What's the use?"

It's of no use, even if we are not alone.

Why then?

Ecclesiastes says, "Whatsoever thy hand findeth to do, do it with thy might, for that is thy portion."

MARCOULE AND GENEVA, OR A FORTNIGHT OF FASTING

Much water has flowed under the bridge since the events at the beginning of the summer of 1958, and it requires some effort to return to them. But we owe our friends an account of them, for several have only heard of our activity through vague echoes in the press.

Besides, it may be good to take a look objectively at an act which has now become detached from us.

You will remember that after our invasion of the Marcoule plant at the end of our Easter camp, we prepared a public march and endeavored to rouse the district to awareness of the immediate danger presented by the nuclear center, which can already poison the wind and rain without any help from the Bomb or from bomb tests.

While on this subject, I want to answer two objections which have been made to us several times. "Why," we are asked, "do you demonstrate against the atomic bomb rather than against any other kind of bomb? Every weapon, including Cain's club, deserves the same reproof."

Such an argument is worthless against nonviolence. Our demonstrating against the Bomb does not mean we approve of other weapons. It is beyond our powers to demonstrate against everything of which we disapprove, but that does not mean we approve of everything against which we do not demonstrate.

Another criticism is, "Why do you kick at the atomic bomb when the peaceful uses of atomic disintegration are scarcely less destructive and dangerous?"

That is what we have kept stating and demonstrating.

But demonstrations of this kind can only touch those who read our writings, listen to our talks, are capable of reasoning and want to understand instead of shutting their eyes. They are inaccessible to the great number (and how many of the tremendously intelligent join the great number by serving as their mouthpieces).

Why, in public demonstrations aimed at touching the conscience of as many people as possible, do we focus attention on the Bomb?

Because the Bomb is the monster's head and we must aim at the head.

Everybody can see plainly that this head, belching forth fire, venom, and death, is the head of a monster. The rest of the body is no less monstrous, but people are too frivolous and silly to notice. They admire the scales on its tail because they glitter and its joints because they are strong.

For public nonviolent action the motive must be simple and obvious.

The Bomb provides such a motive.

The Bomb is not an isolated phenomenon. Its roots, ramifications, and implications ultimately affect the whole of our civilization, of which it is one of the most characteristic and accomplished, and therefore inevitable, fruits. It is not necessary that all those whom we urge to resist its manufacture should grasp the details of this network of causes.

During the whole of April, May, and June, the Companions (both men and women) went every evening in twos and threes and visited farmers, shopkeepers, priests, and mayors, as well as workmen and engineers in Marcoule. Meanwhile, Shantidas went and spoke in local townhalls, traveling as far as Orange, Carpentras, and Avignon.

Submitting to strong pressure from the management of the Marcoule plant, the prefect of the department of Le Gard forbade all meetings and demonstrations by the Ark.

We had intended to lead a public march from Pont-Saint-Esprit (on the boundary of the department) to the gates of Marcoule.

But we gave up this plan, not because of the prefectoral ban (we are not so short of ideas as to have been unable to find some way of getting around it, nor so timid as not to defy it at the risk of being jailed or beaten if that had been fitting).

But events in Algiers, and General de Gaulle's coming into power, had attracted public attention elsewhere. We felt we could not draw enough people together for our protest to carry weight.

We therefore contented ourselves with bringing our sympathizers together at Sénos and devoting the day to a discussion of nonviolence in a more popular style than usual.

Meanwhile, two hundred policemen and their vans were patrolling all the roads leading from Pont-Saint-Esprit to Marcoule and demonstrating in our stead.

There remained that part of the action which was up to us alone—the fast.

We published the following leaflet:

Eighteen of us are going to undertake a complete fast for a fortnight from the thirtieth of June onward. Some of us will camp in front of the Palace of Nations at Geneva, the others beside the atomic energy plant at Marcoule in France.

At the Palace of Nations there will be a conference of experts to study means of controlling nuclear explosions with a view to reaching agreement on the stoppage of tests.

Meanwhile, at Marcoule, preparations for the first French plutonium bomb are being accelerated in view of an impending test in the Sahara.

The least we can do is to offer up this fortnight of suffering and waiting in order to make each and all reflect on this matter of life and death for everybody. Although we have neither power nor authority, we have demands to make for the sake of life, and that is why we feel obliged to fast.

Our fast represents the waiting and the suffering of all the world in front of these buildings in which the life and death of all of us is being discussed, and the death of every one of us premeditated and prepared.

The next nuclear conflagration means hundreds of millions of victims, some of whom will be killed instantly, others condemned for years on end to die a lingering death; as for which people will have to suffer the most, "That," say the experts, "depends on the direction of the wind."

The tests are not a danger: they are a calamity in them-

selves. They raise tons of death-carrying dust which will take
years to settle and will fall on generations to come.

Atomic tests are the war we wage on our children born
and unborn.

That is the simple truth which cannot be denied.

In face of this truth, it does not matter whether one is
right or wrong, strong or weak, the victor or the vanquished.

The only thing that matters is to open your eyes to the
obvious: before us, just two steps farther, opens the abyss.

And on the Sunday evening, the team for Geneva, with
Shantidas at its head, set off.

The other team, whose leader was Pierre Mohandas,[1] got
ready the following day to take up their position on the field.
At the Pont de Codolet, they sent a man ahead to reconnoiter.
He came back with bad news: the road was barred by police
vans. The men who had gone to set up the camp during the
night and enclose the private ground which had been lent had
been taken away one by one (dragged in the fashion to which
we have now become accustomed) by the police, who had torn
down the tents and broken the fences, which, be it said in passing, was quite illegal.

The fasters, disconcerted, came back to Sénos in order to
discuss the next step. They made up their minds to occupy the
site in order to be arrested.

Toward noon, the night team, released by the police, returned.

The fasters set off for Marcoule again, put up the fences
once more and, at the entrance, a board marked PRIVATE
PROPERTY. Then they sat down and waited. Toward six o'clock
in the evening the police came in force, broke down the new

---

[1] The man chosen to succeed Shantidas, named after Gandhi (Mohandas—
servant of the Ravishing Lord).

fences, and took the men off. Buses passed taking workmen back from Marcoule and the occupants, recognizing the demonstrators, waved to them through the windows.

During this time, the Companions who remained at liberty were setting up a camp at Lamotte, on the other side of the Rhône, on the territory of our department, where the police of Le Gard could not disturb them. There was a broad meadow there, an ancient little church, a post office, and a stone cross—in short, everything they needed. They settled in as soon as released and spent the fortnight there.

The *curé* of Lapalud came and said the offices, and the vaults of the church rang with the same plainsong that had filled them when they were new. The voices of the singers grew feebler as the days went by.

Every morning and every evening, at six o'clock, the fasters stood in a row on the bank facing the road, while vans passed taking men to and from the factory. The drivers would hoot and the workmen wave in friendly greeting.

At Geneva, we were given a very warm welcome. A minister of the Protestant church put a corner of his park at our disposal. It was near the palace and had access to the road. Press and television newsmen from all over the world came and questioned and photographed the campers, while friends belonging to the local group lavished kindness on them.

The newspapermen would begin by asking the questions they were sent to ask and writing their articles. Then, seated on the grass, they would start to ask the questions in which they themselves were interested as men. One of them, for reasons of professional conscience, and no doubt also for his own edification, asked if he could fast with us for a day. Others came back next day with their wives, and sometimes with their children. Gradually, people living on the same street, passersby, and then everybody in the town whose curiosity had been aroused by the newspapers got into the habit of coming to see us.

In the evening, we would light a big fire for open prayer, and the circle grew bigger every day right to the end.

On the first Sunday, through the press and the radio, we invited people of all religious denominations to come and listen to some talks on religious unity and the means of approaching it. Geneva is a crossroads in this respect, and nearly all the religions in the world were represented. During the last days of our fast, we held a meeting of all the groups of Friends of the Ark near the frontier from as far as Lyons and Grenoble.

As time went by, our camp got bigger. Some friends came and fasted with us for the last week, others for the last three days; we also discovered new friends.

There was a broad lawn and beautiful trees refreshed by summer showers—we were in paradise.

Apart from some of us who did not feel very well from time to time and had to lie down, we all bore the ordeal well and even came out of it strengthened, except for Chanterelle in the Marcoule team. Unable to stand from the sixth day onward, she suffered beyond measure.

And the result of it all? As everybody knows, the possessors of the bombs decided by common agreement to stop tests for a year. (At least they said so; although they did not do it. Nevertheless, it was a good sign.) We are not claiming that this was brought about by our fast, but it is certain that the pressure of public opinion from both sides of the Iron Curtain had some effect. Public opinion in France was particularly apathetic and inconsistent, whereas the Germans (yes, the Germans) wondered whether France was asleep and completely unaware.

Whatever the practical consequences have been, and even if

there have been none, our gesture has proved necessary for the honor of the country.

THE PROBLEM OF THE BOMB,
OR THE DISINTEGRATION OF LOGIC

According to physics, nuclear disintegration is brought about by a chain of reactions.

The atomic problem causes a similar chain of reactions in the integrity of human reason and will, striking the nations with a mental illness which affects the very nucleus of their faculties.

Every component of the Bomb is a marvel of logic, knowledge, sagacity, foresight, inventiveness, and constructive skills; the whole ends in a senseless and disastrous explosion.

In the same manner, each of the motives which have led to its manufacture has proved irresistible; each of the arguments which defend its necessity, irrefutable; it is not until you consider its purpose that its madness is suddenly apparent.

There is no point in crying out against the accumulation of such devices as a mortal danger and a stupid crime, if we do not recognize the faultless, uninterrupted chain of normal reactions, traditional reasons and precautions which push men to this extremity.

It is a pitfall for logic (a trick of the devil, and the most devilishly clever rush into it).

No doubt it is imprudent to be less strongly armed than neighboring powers. It is probably even more imprudent than not to be armed at all.

What could be more reasonable than to try and make up for lost time when one is unlucky enough to have been outrun?

But those we catch up with will not want to lose the ground they have gained, and those we pass will want to catch up with us; it stands to reason.

What could be more reasonable than to say to oneself, "If I have the ultimate weapon, my terror-stricken neighbor will think twice and I shall be in no danger of his attacking me or of his putting up any resistance."

He will think twice, certainly, but of what, if not of some means of obtaining the ultimate weapon for himself, for the same reasons.

Yes, but what could be more reasonable than that each side should have deterrent weapons, to use the excessively smooth language of our strategists and politicians? They also talk about the "balance of terror," and they found our security on it.

And that is how our economists, so precise and strict where expenditure is concerned, and our men of finance, so attentive to gain, and our technicians, so anxious about stepping up production, and our statesmen, forever trembling lest the budget be in the red, put millions and billions of dollars into the manufacture of arms for the purpose of rendering them useless. What could be more reasonable?

For is not the "balance of terror" our last chance of peace? But to speak of the "balance of terror" is like speaking of the roundness of a square or the whiteness of black.

"Fear is the beginning of wisdom," it has been said. It is true—fear of making a mistake, for example, or fear of offending one's neighbor, fear of God, yes. But terror is the root of the obscurest forms of madness.

Considering that the only defense against this weapon is its equal, each thinks he is protecting himself by becoming more threatening the more he is threatened. It is a vicious circle, a whirlpool from which there is no way out, apart from death.

Every power that lets itself be sucked into the whirlpool drags a series of others with it, including the one it least desires to see rush into its orbit: its worst enemy. And the greater the number of nations holding the privilege of bursting the earth asunder, the greater the number of risks.

Supposing that, because of a false alarm or a misunderstanding, panic seizes the neighboring people or some rather
excitable head of state, and that he convinces himself that before midnight we are going to make a surprise attack, will he
not try to strike us first and wipe us out at a single blow?

But even if those bent on war resist the first temptation, will
they manage to resist the last? Is it impossible that the loser, in
a fit of desperate rage, should throw down his trump card?
Can one doubt for a single moment that when Hitler in his
underground rat-hole fired into his temple and gave himself up
to the flames, he did not feel the baleful joy of dragging the
whole world with him in his fall?

A British Minister of National Defence recently declared,
without any beating around the bush, that there is no possible
defense against nuclear attack. The only assurance he could
give the nation was that an automatic mechanism would immediately give the enemy measure for measure. He concluded this
historic speech by thanking the population for taking it all so
well.

He might well do so, for if I were to die pulverized I doubt
whether I should be consoled by this posthumous revenge on
innocent millions.

But once again, you may say, it is not a question of revenge,
but of protection. The enemy, knowing he cannot escape the
return blow, even if he utterly destroys us, will take good care
not to attack us, and the innocent will be safe on both sides.

I am not so sure. If the return blow depends on a delicate
mechanism, suddenly and easily set off, this apparatus must
constantly be guarded by some technicians. Supposing the enemy
has bribed one of them to cut the wires, he can be sure (rightly
or wrongly) that the return blow will not come, and all the
malice and cleverness of our formidable equipment will be vain
and ridiculous.

But the mechanism might also be set off without malice,

cleverness, or reason aforethought, through a mere technical failure. And it is also possible that something slightly maladjusted might cause us to hit a peaceful neighbor or an ally, or ourselves.

Gribouille was a village idiot who, to shelter from the rain, plunged into the duck pond. He was a forerunner and the head of the school of thought to which our strategists, politicians, valiant defenders, and advanced rulers belong.

But whatever one may expect or fear from terror the day it strikes the nations, and from the frantic activity that will result, there is nothing more alarming than the present total lack of fear, the indifference and insensitivity of the masses. "For as in the days that were before the flood," says Jesus (Matthew 24:38), "they were eating and drinking, marrying and giving in marriage . . . and knew not till the flood came and took them . . ."

"Seers, see not!" they cry, as they did to Isaiah. "Prophets, prophesy not unto us right things, speak unto us smooth things."

People yawn as they look at the pictures of Hiroshima; Japan is so far away. The pleas of Einstein and Schweitzer make them shrug their shoulders. "What can *we* do? The best thing to do is to stop thinking about it. Let's go and look for some entertainment!"

Among other entertainments, let us applaud rockets hurled into the sky, admire the wisdom of those who want to live on the moon, after having made the earth uninhabitable. Let us hope that science and technology will produce excellent vegetables, as a precaution against the time when they will have poisoned everything the earth produces in its present coarse and primitive way.

Let us listen to the clever politicians who teach us that the more bombs we have in reserve, the more peace we shall have.

Let us listen confidently to the scientist on duty whose role it is to persuade us that "every precaution has been taken to save the population" and, above all, to the theologian who explains that it is all orthodox, that one cannot find a single argument in St. Thomas's work against nuclear weapons and that it would be unwise to put forward objections to the doctrine of "just war."

Indeed, war is so just that it is doubly just, just on both sides.

And if you have any doubts, soldier, refrain, refrain from thinking, and hit out!

"For nation shall rise against nation, and kingdom against kingdom: and there shall be famines, and pestilences, and earthquakes, in divers places. All these are the beginning of sorrows" (Matthew 24:7-8).

When the explosion took place at Hiroshima, there was dazzling light and the whole of the city center was blasted in a lightning flash.

There rose from the town such a violent wind that it tore the clothing off the survivors. The women who were wearing kimonos found themselves naked, with the pattern of the cloth seared into their flesh, now decorated with burns. The wind machine-gunned their bodies with stinging fire. Hundreds of thousands of people were consumed in an instant, others took decades to die. To escape from the burning ground, some threw themselves into the river, but the water of the river was boiling.

". . . upon the earth distress of nations, with perplexity; the sea and the waves roaring. Men's hearts failing them for fear . . ." (Luke 21:25).

The 500,000 tons of nitric acid which an H-bomb produces, the 2,000,000 tons of dust it raises, cut off the light of the sun. A thousand such bombs would hide the sun forever and make the earth a dead planet.

"And there shall be signs in the sun, and in the moon, and in the stars . . . for the powers of heaven shall be shaken" (Luke 21:25–26).

"For in those days shall be affliction, such as was not from the beginning of the creation which God created unto this time, neither shall be" (Mark 13:19).

"After all," some people say, "perhaps it is God's will that the earth should perish," and they speak with smiling serenity which would be sublime if it sprang from detachment from all things.

But the people who with such spiritual grandeur envisage the end of all creation in a flood of fire are terrified at the idea of losing ther jobs or being disapproved of by their housekeeper or being taken for bad citizens (by protesting against the Bomb, for example).

Their imagination and common sense are so feeble that they are even incapable of sheer animal fear. They go where they are driven, like cattle to the slaughterhouse, with the difference that they philosophize on the way, and the difference that no animal builds a slaughterhouse or forges a knife to cut its own throat.

"So that, having eyes, they see not and having ears, they hear not . . ."

"And God hardened Pharaoh's heart."

Virgil says, "Whom Jupiter wants to destroy, he first makes mad."

Until such time as one out of the millions of the scatterbrained blows it all up by mistake.

PRESTIGE, HONOR, AND THE BOMB

"It's true," people will say, "that the first atomic bomb destroyed 300,000 people at one blow, but many more than 300,000 were killed without any scandal by non-atomic bombs on different occasions. The number has nothing to do with it.

"If we give up the Bomb, we must also give up cannons, guns, and swords. But there will still be enough stones left to slaughter our neighbor with."

Some will tell us this in order to point out how impossible and ridiculous any endeavor to disarm men even partially would be, seeing that war is inevitable, therefore necessary, not to say salutary and glorious. Others, because they look on war as a crime, find it impossible and ridiculous not to demand total, immediate disarmament.

Our answer to the latter is that total, immediate disarmament cannot be imposed, and that even if it could by chance be imposed, it could not be carried out, since one can kill and be killed not only with stone, water, fire, a bread knife, or an incense burner, but also with the tongue, hatred and contempt, or indifference.

To give up all weapons, one must first and foremost give up wanting to kill. Consequently, disarmament cannot be the first step. It is the second. The first step is argeement. I am not saying harmony or love, but am limiting it to this barest of necessities, short of which nothing can be done.

Total disarmament would be such a disavowal of our agelong habits and attitudes that one cannot dream of accomplishing it at one go. It must be brought about little by little. It is already a step forward to be able to hope for a first step.

The first step is obviously the one for which every reasonable being must recognize the necessity, and on which he cannot refuse to feel the urgency of agreement, under penalty of death.

That is why we insist on abolition of the Bomb, which does not at all imply our approval of other arms.

He who said that whoever lives by the sword shall perish by the sword did not wait for the invention of the Bomb to condemn war and show that it carries its own punishment.

As for those who justify war, we shall not contest the strength

of their main argument, which is that of "legitimate defense."
We shall not call a man a murderer if, attacked by surprise at
night, he can find no better way of saving his life than to kill
his aggressor. We shall not deny that a raving madman who
fires on every passerby should be shot, if that is the only way to
prevent him from doing more harm. But what we do strongly
affirm is that these are accidental cases, exceptional cases, extreme cases, and we should be very wary of setting them up as
examples and deducing general rules from them, much less
theories of legitimacy.

Most human conflict presents itself quite differently, is open
to legal or moral—in short, to human—solution, whereas to
give blow for blow until the stronger gets the better of the other
is of the order of animal reflexes and has nothing to do with
rightness or reason.

In the case of war, who is the aggressor? Each says it is the
other, to such good purpose that the Ministry of War is now
called the Ministry of "National Defense." If everybody is
defending himself, where does the attack come from? asks
Tolstoy. If we begin by justifying defense, we shall be led to
justifying attack as a preventive measure, or as an answer to
provocation, or as revolt against the oppressor or as the recapture
of some possession that has been snatched from us.

Or to snatch from our neighbor some possession of his that
we need or that he doesn't need or that he has wrongly acquired.

Or to defend our honor, fulfill our obligations, and support
our prestige.

Or to draw attention from the scandals of the political setup,
solve the unemployment problem, and turn our domestic enemies
against the foreigner.

To found peace on justice and justice on force . . .

And while the chain of fury and horror lengthens, link by
link, that of justification doubles and reinforces it.

To which there is nothing to be said, unless that the reasons are too good. So good that there is no cause that is not justified and no atrocity that is not justified by the justice of the cause. And this mass of justifications, so well bonded that not one of them can be challenged, entirely covers up God's fifth commandment:

THOU SHALT NOT KILL

which was given on a tablet of stone without margins so that no interpretation could be added to it.

Wherefore, instead of putting their interpretation beside it, or under it, they have put it over it, and in place of the commandment, there are now all the contrary doctrines and recommendations.

In consequence of which war comes as a scourge.

A man-made scourge.

And everyone knows that it is chastisement sent by God.

How can one tell that it is sent by God? From the fact that the guilty inflict it on themselves with zeal and obstinacy, adapting it each as it befits him.

There are two ways of breaking the chain of legitimate violence, the violence that finds its justification in the adversaries' wrongs.

One is *perpetual warfare*, as history proves—and now, with the coming of total war and the ultimate weapon, *total destruction.*

The other is to break the chain, in other words, liberation, or conversion, or nonviolence.

The way preached by the Gospel, and five centuries earlier by Buddha, and ten centuries before Buddha, by Joseph, son of Jacob Israel, the spiritual way demonstrated by the tradition of saints, wise men, and prophets, while in our own century of utmost peril, Gandhi has shown its practical application.

He has shown how resistance by the force of the spirit (for

Satyagraha is indeed a matter of power and struggle, and not of resignation and acquiescence) can repulse an invader, even if he is a thousand times better armed and has been deeply entrenched in the country for more than a hundred years.

He has proved that the force of spirit can uplift a downtrodden class, as has been shown by the liberation of the untouchable pariahs—that in a few days, it can put an end to a war, since the massacres of Hindus and Pakistanis were abruptly halted (1947).

Justice requires that we should fight for it unto death, but these historic examples open the way to other forms of combat and teach us that recourse to war, questionable at all times, and today disastrous, no longer serves any purpose.

Having said that, and briefly told you what I really think, let me return to the first point—I mean, the Bomb—and confront those who refuse to follow me to this conclusion, and stick to the reasonable, traditional argument that weapons are justified by the necessity for war and war by the necessity for defense.

If that were true, and in the day of Queen Victoria it was still possible to think so, the fact remains that nuclear weapons are of a different species from all others. The number of victims and amount of damage are not the only considerations. There are thresholds beyond which quantitative difference changes the very quality of things and the nature of problems.

If war is acceptable up to a certain point, as a defense, a lesser evil, as the advantage of the greater good expected from it over the immediate and certain evil it does, armament is likewise acceptable only as a balance between offensive and defensive weapons.

During the Middle Ages, said to be times of barbarism, but times of heroic lay and legend, the superiority of defensive weapons was remarkable.

But the offensive weapons of the period are almost as rudimentary (apart from their form and decoration) as those of cave dwellers. Slings, bows and arrows, clubs, axes, swords, lances were almost all there were.

But what technical marvels and what inventive genius went into defense! Coats of mail, cuirassas complete for man and horse, visored helmets, jointed gloves, shields, mobile carapaces one on top of the other, ramparts, double and triple walls, moats, bulwarks, battlements, zigzag passages, barbicans, machicolations, underground galleries and dungeons.

The rider was almost invulnerable; to climb ramparts was often impossible. Citadels and castles had to be reduced by famine or taken by treachery. A historic battle ended with a few dozen dead. The enemy, overthrown, was taken prisoner, released for a ransom, and often set free on parole. War was still something of a tournament, the game sometimes fatal, but only by accident. It was a trial of valor and self-mastery.

With the cannon and musket came the predominance of offensive weapons (and the virtues of chivalry immediately fell into disrepute). The armor collapsed, walls crumbled. Man eventually presented his chest bare to the grapeshot, his only defense a chance of passing between the bullets and the cannonballs; his buckler, the rank of men in front of him.

The First World War brought about the relinquishing of all defense except the most elementary, which was to entrench oneself, or throw oneself face downward into holes and hollows in the ground.

The troops attacked in waves, their rampart and ramp, hundreds of thousands of corpses.

Toward the end, a perilous tin hat made its appearance as a protection against stray bullets and falling debris of metal and stone, and during the last months, there were tanks to take the trenches by force.

Between the two wars, a great deal of defensive equipment

was built on the basis of faulty ideas and outdated strategic theory. The Maginot Line was built, or rather buried. But at the first attack, the new Wall of China crumbled like a sand castle in the rising tide. Enemy planes swept over it with the greatest of ease, dropped troops by parachute, and took it from the rear.

The same fate overtook the blockhouses of the Atlantic Wall and the Siegfried Line in turn.

Even the combined military forces could no longer protect the homefront now exposed to air raids and long-range shelling. The only defense possible was "passive" and consisted of sheltering in cellars, firing at planes, or giving them chase.

And none of this will be of any use against rockets, and even underground shelters will provide no protection against atomic bombing, should the latter pollute for any length of time the surface from which we must draw breath and nourishment.

The sword is a noble weapon.

Only its point is for attack. The rest of it is for defense.

The Bomb is the vilest of weapons, forbidden by definition, since there is no defense against it.

If defense is what makes combat legitimate, the ultimate weapon against which there is no defense is all offense and totally evil.

What is totally evil is also mad.

It is conceivable that a man should sacrifice himself for his land and his home, but if at the same time he sacrifices that for which he is sacrificing himself, his act is no longer a sacrifice, but suicide and an unpardonable crime.

To die in nuclear war is to die three times over: it is to die oneself, to die in one's children, and to die with the whole of nature.

. . .

My friends! look up quickly, look up at the sky while it is still blue!

Touch the earth before it crumbles.

Run to the spring and drink before it is poisoned, bathe in the sea before it is polluted.

But above all, enjoy your children at play before they fall sick, before their blood turns bad, before they are slowly burned to death.

You're afraid they'll wet their feet, poor little things! You're afraid they'll catch cold. You're afraid they'll fail their exams, poor children!

But the scientific sores that tamperers with atoms are preparing for them don't worry you in the the least, do they?

We are at a turning point in history, where France might have played her part.

We do not believe in "France's nuclear vocation"; we believe in her chivalrous vocation.

The means of wholesale destruction is the direct opposite of every chivalrous virtue.

Mechanical annihilation of the enemy, by remote control and without even seeing him—men, women, and old people alike— is directly opposed to all justice, all honor, and all glory.

Prestige indeed! Plotting this heinous crime in cold blood is the mark of the greatest cowardice and vileness, of cunning inspired by terror—blind cunning, moreover, since it falls into its own trap!

Blessed are those who do not have this temptation; more blessed still those who are able to resist it out of spiritual strength or simple common sense.

Those who have no bomb are also those who have the most chance of being safe from it, whatever people say.

For if conflict breaks out between a power which has nuclear weapons and another which has not, it is very likely that the power which has nuclear force will stick to traditional weapons, as was the case in the Korean War, although it was not possible to win a decisive victory.

The weaker the adversary's arms, the more likely this is.

Even the most ambitious and inhuman of conquerors cannot find the slightest advantage in reigning over distintegrated peoples or annexing a radioactive desert.

Speaking of victory or defense with the aid of atomic weapons is behind the times. It is believing in the good old days of Stonewall Jackson.

The future belongs to the nations that have no Bomb. Moreover, they are in the majority, and form the stock of future generations.

Will they be clearsighted enough to perceive that it is an honor, an advantage, and an insurance? Will they be capable of standing up to the destroyers, disintegrators, and dissuading them?

Who can speak on their behalf, defend and unite them, become their savior if not a power which, although it could have the ultimate weapon, refuses to use it? Only a power which has it and then gives it up.

France could play this vitally important role.

Is she going to go on ruining herself just to keep up her position of last among the great, the clay pot between two iron pots, arousing suspicion and hatred on all sides, rushing into toil, disappointment, and danger for the sole purpose of claiming the right to a share in the great destruction?

Or is she going to be intelligent enough, free enough, courageous enough to undertake the mission that will make her praised and blessed by the whole world and future generations?

3

AGAINST INTERNMENT CAMPS

THE LARZAC EXPEDITION

June 1959

It all began at Le Vigan with a lecture given by Jo Pyronnet, a philosophy teacher; at the end of the lecture he asked his audience to do some charitable act, such as going to the aid of the recently opened Camp du Larzac nearby, where he knew that some of the prisoners were in dire need.

From the charitable act as a measure of emergency, he went on to nonviolent action, that is to say, consideration of the root of the problem. He determined to find out first, what the camp was, who its prisoners were, why and how they had been imprisoned, and lastly, whether they could not be helped with regard to their greatest loss, namely, freedom.

He soon found out that under the name "Camps d'Assignation à Résidence Surveillée" ("Supervised Resident Assignment Camps") he was dealing with an institution we got to know well during the German occupation: the concentration camp. The German ones began like this. Enemies, or supposed enemies, of the regime were shut up in them to prevent their doing harm, and it ended with gas chambers and ovens. People will object that France is well known for her humanity and that some things are impossible here. The argument would be much more reassuring if the innumerable and unspeakable atrocities committed by the French police and the French army in Indochina, Madagascar, Morocco, Tunisia, Algeria, and France could still be ignored.

Today[1] there are four concentration camps in France being filled with more and more Algerians picked up in police raids or as they come out of prison. Tomorrow, they may be filled with Frenchmen of one kind or another, according to the politics of the government in power.

On the twenty-eighth of June, at the end of the Assembly for the Feast of St. John at the Community of the Ark, sixty people proceeded to the Larzac plateau. The day began with Mass. The procession formed at the church door in La Cavalerie and marched past the barbed wire of the camp, between two rows of state police, holding their revolvers.

The march brought no reaction from the public authorities, and so seven volunteers came forward to the entrance of the camp, and asked to be interned. "We also are Frenchmen with full rights[2] and we also have every right to be called 'suspect' since a suspect is somebody against whom no precise accusation can be made."

But here the nonviolent met with an unexpected obstacle—the nonviolence of the police, and the camp management, who pointed out to them that they could only be interned by order of the ministry, courteously ordered them to withdraw, then begged and finally implored them not to prolong an embarrassing and useless discussion. It therefore seemed more gallant

[1] 1959.
[2] At the time, the French government pretended that Algerians were "Frenchmen with full rights."

and decent to give in, and the seven went to join the main body of the protesters at Millau. These were advancing, with their banners displayed, through the Sunday street toward the prefecture. The police soon took their placards away from them and barred the streets. So the demonstrators sat down on the sidewalk. Among them were three inhabitants of the town (four, if we include a novice from the Ark), one of whom was a well-known personality. It was all the more to his credit that he sat on the sidewalk with us, to the astonishment of his fellow citizens.

There was another conversation with the police, who treated us very kindly. They finally said that under no circumstances would they use force and that they would remain on duty as long as necessary, but they begged us, for charity's sake, to cut the demonstration short. Once more, the nonviolent, who would not have resisted ill-treatment, were beaten with their own arms.

This day bore fruit. Many members of the public spontaneously took part in our action, and among the police there were some who discovered nonviolence, its strength and its beauty. A police officer whose duty it was to make inquiries confessed he had not slept for two nights because his encounter with nonviolence had stirred his conscience as never before in his life.

Naturally we did not want to withdraw after this "stalemate" (as far as exterior results were concerned). The action is going on and will probably keep us in a state of alert for the rest of the year.

To begin with, at the end of July, Jo, Daniel, our Companion Piéra, and a group of friends are going on a nine-day fast in front of the camp. Meanwhile the following letter has been sent to the Ministry of Home Affairs in conformity with the legal procedure the head of the camp told us to follow when he gave his reasons for refusing to let in the volunteers.

Castelnau-le-Lez
July 9, 1959

Open letter to Mr. X:
Minister of Home Affairs

The undersigned, to
Mr. X, Minister of Home Affairs
Mr. Y, Sub-Prefect of Millau
Mr. Z, Prefect of Rodez

Sir,

As men, and Frenchmen, we feel deeply affected in our conscience, our honor, and dignity by the creation and development of internment camps in France. The fact that thousands of mere suspects are shut up in these camps for "official" reasons has taken all the enjoyment out of our freedom and made it meaningless. So, in order to share in the injustice being done to our Algerian brothers, and as a sequel to the protest made on the twenty-eighth of June in front of the Larzac Camp, we feel compelled to request our voluntary internment in that or any other camp or prison you care to choose. We wish to be considered also as suspects fit to be put on your blacklist, and we are placing ourselves at your disposal to fill the places still vacant in these camps whenever you think fit. It matters little to us on which side of the barbed wire we are, if the price of our freedom is the freedom of our brothers.

Rest assured that in acting thus we are yielding to the pressure of our conscience only, and not to any order or maneuver of a political nature.

Yours respectfully,

DANIEL WINTREBERT
JO PYRONNET

[both residing at Castelnau-le-Lez, Hérault]

The list of volunteers is open!

It is a question now of two things: that a sufficient number of French citizens should prove their love of their country's freedom by volunteering for imprisonment; secondly, if their written request does not produce satisfactory results, that they should act in such a way as to assert their right to imprisonment, that is to say, that they should enter into civil disobedience until the wicked decree is abolished.

THE THIRTY AT THOL

Friends of the Ark will know about the Satyagraha in the spring of 1960 from the reports that appeared in the press. It created a bigger stir than our previous campaigns had done. Thanks to that, the word "nonviolence" began to appear in the headlines, backed up by photographs, as well as in police reports, cartoons, and newsreels. Nonviolence became a subject of passionate polemics and provided some very intelligent people with an opportunity of saying some remarkably silly things, and the *Canard Enchaîné* (a humorous, satirical newspaper) with the chance to make an appropriately serious reply; it brought about uneasy curiosity in some and conversion in others. But I am not sure that from all the news items and discussions published there emerges a vivid enough picture or a clear enough sense of the adventure, so I shall try to give both in this account of it.

It began with the nonviolence camp opened this year at Grézieux, near Lyons. Bright, chilly days in the meadow under the apple trees in blossom. About 150 friends. Jo Pyronnet gave a talk on truth and life, Hegnauer on nonviolence and fear, Jean Goss on the appeals he had made under the golden ceilings of the Vatican and on the Red Square in Moscow on behalf of nonviolence; Shantidas on the true holy war, which is the defense of righteousness with the weapons of righteousness.

The thirty volunteers were there. Twenty-five belonged to

the Ark (nineteen friends and allies, five Companions and a novice). It was their starting point and vigil of arms. Their conference around a long table was wonderful to see. It would have been difficult to invent such a diversity of class, race, religion, character, and appearance. Yet nonviolence had soon given them a "family resemblance," as they say.

Nothing was missing from the day's preparation, which was to be the tenth of April, not even a visit from the police to tell us that all demonstrations in the neighborhood of Thol were forbidden. This fell in with our plans. The fact is that when a demonstration is allowed by those against whom it is directed, it is because they consider it unimportant and ineffective. Besides, it should be remembered that the nonviolent demonstrators had not only demanded the abolition of prison camps, but had proposed becoming prisoners themselves so as to lend weight to their demand, and they were prepared to break the law in order to obtain satisfaction. Now it is not always easy to break the law without harming or offending somebody. The opponent's arbitrary decrees and acts of violence are a great help in avoiding this difficulty.

The sun rose in a clear sky on this Palm Sunday. Friends from Grenoble and Annecy were to join those from Grézieux and Lyons at Pont-d'Ain, a small town near the Thol Camp.

"To be sure, it is a fine thing to commemorate Christ's Passion by reading the Bible and by attending Mass," said the priest from Grenoble who was in the pulpit. "But it is better still to share in it by suffering persecution for righteousness' sake, as those who are going to the Thol Camp are about to do." And he himself went there with three other priests and some parishioners.

The demonstrators, two hundred of them, marched through the square and out of the village in silence, banners unfurled. But when they had passed the last houses, they were confronted by a police block. The police ordered them to disperse and took their placards away. They all sat down. It was noon and the Sunday sun was ablaze. The gendarmes cast questioning looks at one another, shouted orders right, left, and center, police on motorcycles shot off to bring reinforcements and instructions. The nonviolent demonstrators waited calmly. They felt strength on their side. For many of them, this was the first time. Some had "just come to see." They got what they wanted. From that very moment, they were given a taste of what nonviolence was all about. It was worth more than ten years of reading and reflection on the subject.

It took the police two hours to carry the demonstrators into the police vans. But conversation had already begun between the police and the public.

"The Algerians are perfectly well fed and well treated in the camps. They're better off than at home."

"What do you need the barbed wire for then? And the machine guns and the watchtowers and the police dogs? Why don't you just leave the doors open and let them go in by themselves?"

"What have you got against the camps?"

"You put people into them without judging them."

"They're dangerous, some of them are killers."

"Prove it then! Put them on trial!"

"So you think it would be more just if they'd had a trial?"

"*You're* saying that! If you're saying it yourself, and that's your opinion of the justice you're serving, we have nothing to add."

At last the vans moved off, and six kilometers farther on dumped us in a field of daisies.

The procession formed again, skirted the policemen who were guarding the road, by marching alongside it without leaving the meadow, and headed for Pont-d'Ain while the thirty, walking rapidly ahead, passed the village and started on the road to Thol. But the police drove them back to the square, their starting point, as if they wanted to attract as much attention as possible to the demonstration they were preventing.

There was no lack of spectators in their Sunday best. Opinions differed, and arguments were going strong. The mayor, in the front row, was foaming at the mouth and screaming, "Throw them into the river! Bash them, kill them! I'll have none of that here!" He was like a dog barking while wagging his tail, overjoyed at being able to work himself into a fit of righteous anger.

But Jo Pyronnet, leader of the thirty, having given his men a moment's respite on the portico of the church, reminded them briefly of their aim, and that they must keep calm and obey orders. "Let's go," he cried finally, and moved forward. But the police sergeant for whom "orders" were those of keepers of peace, flung out his arms and shouted, "I order you to stop!" He was outraged to see that the demonstrators ignored him, and a scuffle ensued.

It was no longer a question of sitting on the ground as in the morning, but of marching on the Thol Camp; nevertheless, jostled and kicked, we found ourselves on the ground once more. We were then thrown into the police vans. But those who had fallen on the sidewalk got up again, and those who had been shoved into the vans jumped out, and the blows began to fall thick and fast.

"That's the leader! Grab him! Hold him!" No sooner was this done than somebody else raised his head and shouted, "I'm the leader!" And he had his Companions behind him and police on top of him. Each of us was leader in turn, long enough to be knocked down.

Roger, who had received some hard blows on the right, looked at his gendarme and said, "Well, is that all?" And he received what was due to him on the left, obeying the rule of turning the other cheek.

Big Joseph, his rib cage almost smashed in, nearly exploded, but contained himself, then he did explode. Raising both fists toward heaven, he shouted: "I—I—I love you, my neighbor!"

"You dirty b——!" howled a bloated red face contorted with fury. "We'll do you in!" And for the third time, he threw the leader of the group into the van and hit him as if to reduce him to his smallest bulk once and for all. But as soon as the prisoner could free his hands, he stooped to pick something up and handed it to the gendarme, saying: "I think you've lost something." The gendarme recognized his watch, which had fallen in the struggle, took it, turned away, and took his cap off to mop his brow.

Meanwhile the main body of the demonstrators had arrived, in time to see the last of the thirty being taken away. When the demonstrators had been removed, there was nothing else for the friends to do but return to their cars and go home.

Man proposes, God disposes, as they say. Those of us who were prepared to go to prison were given the punishment of complete freedom and were scattered in the open countryside in the middle of the night.

Next day it rained. Holy Week had begun, it was evening, and they were on foot, and alone. There were no longer friends to keep them company and support them, nor spectators who, even if indifferent, oblige a man to put up a brave front. This time, they approached the camp from another side. They avoided the road patrols, not because of any clever maneuvering but by mistake, because they had gotten lost on the way. And now, what would they meet with? Truncheons? Machine guns? Dogs let loose at their throats? And instead of the friendly gendarmes at Pont-d'Ain, the uniformed toughs of the state police?[3]

[3] The notorious and feared "C.R.S."

. . .

Yes, it was just that; there they were, in front of the first huts. It was all over very quickly, much more quickly and, to tell the truth, much more gently than the previous day. They found themselves in the yard of the gendarmerie at Pont-d'Ain, that is to say, on familiar ground.

The gendarmes remembered that they were civil servants and zealously performed their function—which is to proliferate useless formalities. They lined the delinquents up against the wall as if they were going to shoot them, announced that they would search them and went through the motions of doing so. Then, they sat down at a table and took down everyone's particulars, although their identity had scarcely changed since the day before, and recorded the statements of the demonstrators which also had not changed; the latter pleaded guilty to having knowingly and deliberately infringed the prefectorial decrees, to twice having disturbed the peace by forbidden demonstrations, to having resisted the police, etc. Moreover, they affirmed that they intended to repeat these offenses, and finally demanded that they should undergo the penalties laid down by law.

But the way of the law, as observed, is not so easily foreseen, and logic is no help. They were made to sleep in a garage, so determined were the gendarmes to avoid every appearance of internment or legal punishment.

Next day, they were shown the door and told they could go shopping, but they protested that the police must feed them since they had arrested them. But once again, logic didn't work, and they had to share the remains of yesterday's snack among them, and each got an inch of bread and an inch of cheese. Then thus restored, they filled the yard of the gendarmerie with the sound of singing:

> *Thirty men we were*
> *Thirty thieves together*
> *All clad in white . . .*[4]

[4] A popular seventeenth-century song.

The policemen's wives were at their windows; the singers were soon surrounded with children, and the men, too, drew near—the same men who had dragged and hit them the day before, and they began to chat and take part in the fun and ask questions.

When evening came, the prisoners were told to climb into trucks, and they thought that they were being taken at last to distant prisons, penitentiaries more suited to their offense. But the countryside stretched into the distance, the air grew fresher, and they were up in mountains. During the night, they were dropped off here and there in the region of Saint-Claude and in the passes of the Jura, from where they returned to Lyons as best they could.

On the Thursday, they held a meeting and decided to observe a truce over Easter, fast for the next two days and keep a night vigil, since the best and certainly the most effective aspect of nonviolent action is the struggle for self-mastery in the sight of God.

On the following day, at the insistence of a reporter friend, they did penance, in the form of a press conference. They had to stand, stomachs empty, in the stuffy room behind their spokesman, answering the questions and objections of friends and enemies, and those who were simply trying to understand. A nonviolent act being testimony of truth, explanation of the act is also an act and a duty.

After that it was clear that the chapter was finished and that when the Holy Days had ended, the next step was to go to Paris and there strike a great blow and endure a greater ordeal, for which they now felt prepared.

THE THIRTY IN PARIS
Easter, 1960

Then the thirty tackled Paris during Easter week, not without some apprehension, for everything connected with the capital, including the white truncheon of the *flic* (the popular, contemptuous word for a French policeman), is impressive.

To be sure, since they had come to claim their share of the treatment dealt out to suspects, they were convinced that this time they would "get satisfaction" (to use the expression in their letter to the ministry); nevertheless, in all things, excess is something to be feared, even excess of satisfaction.

However, the confrontation was not so painful as they had expected. They were constantly rebuffed, but without serious ill-treatment, and sometimes in a fairly civil manner, which induced them to prolong the attempt, and it was this that proved harder to bear than brutality or imprisonment.

In the first place, they no longer had a "home" as they had had in Lyons, that is to say, a place, open at all hours, where they could meet, sleep, eat, wash, and have their headquarters. They also missed the mothering of Christiane, the leader's wife. They were now scattered through the huge metropolis far from each other, lodging with friends, some of whom had children to look after, sleeping on sofas or in corridors where it was difficult to snatch a few hours' sleep in the morning after the adventures of the night. It took hours of traveling for the group to gather, just before the attack, on the third floor at the end of the third yard off the number 253 in the sordid rue St. Denis where the open plot, the plot without secrets, was being laid.

There, Jo, the leader, consulted his band of men about what action to take, the dangers and blunders to avoid, until they came to a unanimous and spontaneous decision, which was the one he had arrived at the night before, all by himself.

Not that he brought them round to his way of thinking by wrangling or cleverness of any kind. Built like a Roman legionary, the man, with his gruff way of speaking, is a born leader, and the magic of the leader, nonviolent or otherwise, is to express and consummate the will of one and all in his own will without infringing their freedom.

The thirty arrrived at their destination without being stopped, which they had never been able to do at Thol. Their goal was the sorting camp at Vincennes where they asked to see the man in charge. He did not respond but sent police cars instead, and the thirty soon met again at the police station, or rather, twenty-nine of them did, for one of them was missing—Hamdani, the Algerian.

When young Hamdani (who had spent the whole year at the Ark in Sénos) had proposed to take part in the Satyagraha, the others did their best to dissuade him, fearing that he would run a much greater risk than they. Then, as he persisted in his resolve, they were forced to admit his right as an Algerian to take upon himself his share of tribulation for his brothers on both sides. All felt the symbolic value of his presence in their ranks, so they tutored him and watched over him. They were glad to see that in their first brushes with the police he had not been singled out but had been treated like one of them. And now, what they had feared was happening—he had been discreetly cut off from them due to the confusion when the police had picked them up.

And that was not all: this time, they were presenting themselves without papers so as to have one more reason for being arrested.

They had said so at the very start of the ceremony of identity-checking. What did that matter? The policeman was willing, notebook in hand, to take their word for it—which, by the way, was quite illegal.

"Your name?" he asked the first. But there was no answer.

"What's yours?" he shouted threateningly, marching up to

another who looked more timid; but he got nothing out of him either.

Then Jo, the leader, stepped forward and said, "Write down that we are all named Hamdani."

"Eh? What? What do you mean?"

The timid boy explained, "Hamdani is our Algerian brother, the one you have kept apart."

The leader continued, "Go and tell your superiors that we are all called Hamdani."

And the timid boy added, "You won't get any other answer out of us until you have let him come back."

Hamdani was not allowed to come back, but they were all led into the room where he had been isolated. It boiled down to the same thing, except that the honor of public authority was safe. And now, since one good deed deserves another, they were very happy to give their surnames, Christian names, addresses, and all the rest of it, enough to blacken a whole notebook and delight a policeman's heart.

They came back next day in threes and fours, in order to vary the tactics and prolong the operation, so as not to be taken altogether, and above all, to temper each man's courage more effectually than if they had been sheltered by their own numbers and advancing side by side.

This time, the identification ceremony was a more brilliant affair, since the ministry had sent in a team of investigators. A row of tables the full length of the room, the interrogators on one side, their victims on the other.

"Your name?"

"Courtois."

"Christian name?"

"Christian."

"Profession?"

"Student."

"Father's profession?"

"Officer."

"Ah? Oh! What . . ."

At another table—

"Your name?"

"Lanvin."

"Christian name?"

"Jean-Pierre."

"Profession?"

"Representative of the firm Lanvin."

"Father's profession?"

"Industrialist."

"What? The head of the firm? What are *you* . . ."

But Jean-Pierre was no longer listening. His attention was wholly taken up by the voice at the next table. The tone was over-familiar and aggressive, and the manner of address even more so. Jean-Pierre was just about to say to his interrogator, "Please don't be so polite to me, since your colleague . . ." but before the words could cross his lips Hamdani, jumping to his feet, moved to the other side of the table and in a playful manner, patting the policeman on the back, said as if humoring him, "Here, I'll show you how to write it, I'll write it for you, man, since you don't know how and can't understand . . ."

The policeman got the point. "No, thank you, there's no need to. Sit down. Right, Hamdani with an H, you said. Profession? Home address? . . ." Everything was all right again.

The following day, they let the police wait for them in vain. They had better things to do—a visit to make which they had planned right from the start.

Since the day at Larzac and every time they had come up against the police, the invitation had been repeated: "Go and see the minister! *We* can't do anything about it."

So they went to Place Beauvau.

"Have you an appointment with the minister?" asked the porter.

"And how!" they answered. "He's been expecting us for a long time!"

This was quite enough for the porter. The minister did not rush to meet his guests on the marble staircase but other representatives of the Republic surrounded them eagerly.

And the usual scene took place in unusual surroundings.

The cage in the 8th arrondissement differed from all those they had been in. It was luxurious, painted, and glass-paned. They called it the Aquarium, and it became so familiar to them that they soon felt as at home as fish in water.

That night, they were released later than usual, on Mont-Valérien. Shortly afterward they ran into a squad of gendarmes.

"What are you doing here at this time of night?"

"You should ask the police who brought us here."

"Very fishy. Come with us."

"Oh, very gladly, Messieurs les Gendarmes."

Thinking they were being made fun of, they became annoyed, but as the answers became more and more serious and polite, disconcerted, they asked, "But who *are* you?"

"We are the nonviolent."

"Oh, it's you, is it! That's a bit too much! Clear off! And the quicker the better!"

"How right you are. Our day is finished and so is yours. Time to go to bed."

But their night was not finished. They still had twenty miles to go on foot, through the deserted suburbs, till the first morning bus.

On the morrow, so as to prove the untruth of the rather too popular definition of nonviolence as "sitting on the sidewalk" they chose to stand as long as possible, replacing firmness of foundation by mobility.

And since they were told to "keep moving," they kept moving.

We called it the Corrida—Place Beauvau is round and busy and the name suits it.

As a result, there was some disorder, a few bottlenecks at the pedestrian crossings, a great crowd of amused onlookers, and, not unreasonably, a sudden explosion of temper on the part of our worthy gendarmes which led to a pocket being torn off, some clothes being ripped, and a few tears in the skins in which the Lord wrapped all the sons of Adam.

A well-dressed elderly gentleman with a very distinguished decoration in his lapel was the last to leave, and he concluded, "There are thirty of them today, tomorrow there will perhaps be thirty thousand. When there are thirty thousand of them, no police, no army will be able to withstand them and it will be like Gandhi in India!"

The day after that, there were not thirty thousand of us on the embankment in front of the Château de Vincennes, but we were well over a thousand.

There I found old friends, some of whom I had not seen for fifteen years: Madaule, Marrou, Père Régamey, Pastor Roser, Massignon, Barrat, Domenach, Tresmontant, Théodore Monod, and many others. In those days we would spend the evening discussing philosophy and, among other things, non-violence, and I never imagined or expected that one day we should find ourselves side by side in the field.

When the group of "personalities," as they say, walked into the square, the action had already begun. The demonstrators had sat down on the big square of beaten earth and the police were bustling around them removing banners while press and television cameras were taking aim. Big trucks were maneuvering, and the police had begun to pick people up. We sat down in the dust with the others.

"Come now!" said a police officer to a tall monk with a face carved out of marble and eyes lost in the distance, "come now, Father, don't act like a child!"

As a gendarme was about to grab an old man's legs, one of his colleagues restrained him, "Take care, he's a member of the Institute."[5]

Whereupon the famous professor shot through the air, arms and legs flying, and after him came the black and white monk like a great bird. The photograph of this scene in a newspaper the next day bore the caption, "We've never seen *this* in Paris before."

In the thick of the fighting, some businessman came out of the subway, all dressed for the office. But public authority, rightly considering the joke out of place, barred his way and accosted him.

He replied that he would have nothing to do with such ridiculous goings-on. For this lack of cooperation he was justly rewarded with a beating.

Not being nonviolent, he struggled, for which he got his deserts, a double ration of kicks.

Finally, to overcome his untimely and burdensome neutrality, they grabbed, strapped and whacked him and threw him into their truck.

He arrived among the last in the cellars of the police "commissariat" of the 3rd arrondissement, and his lunatic screaming brought a sudden hush in conversations, introductions, exchanges of visiting cards, cries of surprise from old friends meeting or old enemies falling into one another's arms.

A policeman rebuked him in the calm tones of reason. "Look

---

[5] One of the great Academies of Science.

here, sir, you know perfectly well that violence won't get you anywhere!"

Meanwhile, I was riding, I am proud to say, in the most academic police van the earth has ever borne.

"What do you think, cher ami, of that book that's just come out, *The Gospel and the Labarum,* a Swiss theologian's thesis?"

"It's a good reference book, but there's nothing new in the thesis; everybody knows that the Church had a horror of bloodshed, arms, and armies before the edict of Constantine (which is no doubt the reason why Constantine was not given baptism till he was on his deathbed). But it would be much more interesting, to my mind, to show how this attitude persisted in many respects until the middle of the tenth century, and I learned that from you, Marrou-Davenson"—turning toward him—"ten years ago, at the Congress at ———. A historian of your caliber should now write a sequel to the book, which, by the way, is very well documented and extremely well put together."

The van and the talk ran on. We drove through gates which did not look like prison gates.

They were those of the cemetery at Bagnolet. We were told to get out and were led in procession to the grave of a young police officer recently murdered by an Algerian.

A policeman in civilian dress was spokesman: "Since you call yourselves nonviolent," he said to us, "we should like you to meditate on this victim of violence and duty."

This funeral booby-trap, which several newspapers described as "a good lesson for the nonviolent," was the work of M. Papon, prefect of police of the Seine. As great a philosopher as he is a clever cop, knowing the company he had to deal with, he prided himself, as you see, on beating fine intellectuals at their own game.

We did not feel like playing and observed a few minutes' silence at the poor boy's grave.

As for the subject of meditation he had set us, we had not waited for the order of the prefect of police or his moral guidance to reflect on it.

The equality of death was the conclusion we had arrived at.

And that it behooves us to have no more special delight in one corpse than in another, no more affection for a murder called an assassination than for one called repression, or war, or justice, or pacification.

(However, I must confess that I have a certain weakness for the murder called murder.)

Pastor Roser, after a short speech to this effect, walked back to the gate and asked the police superintendent what he proposed to do with us. "You are free, gentlemen," he said, and added, "I agree with you wholeheartedly." And he went on, his eyes shining with sincerity, "Oh, I do hope you will succeed! If only they would do away with these camps and all the rest of it and let us get back to being what we are, guardians of the peace!"

"Oh," exclaimed the novice Arnaud, "how difficult it is to like you policemen! We have attacked and provoked you fifteen times in succession, and not one of you has become converted yet!"

No, not one of them had become converted, but all were at least tamed, and almost all felt nervous and curious.

Sufficient proof of this was the irresistible urge they felt to come into the cell and argue with demonstrators in order to prove to them that they were "absolutely wrong."

At other times, they came really to talk and even to listen, and sometimes to bring us cans of beer. Finally, a senior officer invited a demonstrator to lunch at his home the following day.

Readers who have any acquaintance whatever with police customs will guess that this was in order to "draw him out." But they were wrong. It was the police officer who let out many secrets and did not attempt to get even one from the demonstrator, knowing for certain that we have none.

However, the struggle was getting tougher. For demonstrators sitting comfortably on the sidewalk or shuffling round and round were things of the past. Now, they used the "tower." This is a war machine which consists of making three circles of ten men facing outward, arms linked, hands clasped on their stomachs.

On their arrival at the police station after the battle demonstrators sometimes received rough congratulations from their opponents.

One day, however, they turned up so unprotected and defenseless that they might have been taken for passersby had they not already been so well known.

Their leader explained. "We heard yesterday about the attack in which one of your men was killed. Out of respect for your bereavement, we shall climb into the vans of our own accord." After a moment, he added, "But first let us observe a minute's silence together." So police and demonstrators stood face to face, in the middle of the street, erect and with their eyes closed.

There was one last operation to complete the cycle. It was their finest, yet it went almost unmentioned in the press.

It took place at the Place de la Concorde (where, in the absence of any news reporters, "forty centuries contemplated" their gesture). Around the obelisk there are green, pointed railings in which there is a little gate. They picked the padlock and locked it again when they had gone inside.

Under the inscription at the base, where you can make out the words "To the applause of an immense people," they hung their banner: *Assignez nous à résidence* (Send us to an internment camp).

And straight and grave as sentinels they stood around the obelisk with their backs to it.

The beautiful spring day was ending and the sun was gilding the square. At that time of day, the traffic is very heavy. It slowed down at first, then, as cars started to go around the obelisk three times in succession, it tripled.

Then it came to a complete standstill. Passersby ran across from the distant sidewalk. At last, the familiar *képis* (police caps) appeared.

All that remained for the demonstrators to do now was vault over the pointed railings.

Then came the day on the Champs-Élysées. They had invited the crowd to follow them to the Ministry of Home Affairs. But the police kept them massed in the busiest of thoroughfares.

The prefect of police came to direct operations in person. Many people made fun of us and disdained to take us seriously. Not so Monsieur Papon, for whom it was no joking matter. The show of force was much greater than at Vincennes, the spectators more numerous but less friendly, for we were not well liked in residential quarters. Distinguished onlookers distinguished themselves by their bad grace. But among the people sitting with us, we also sensed a certain partisan rancor that took precedence over humane considerations. The two Frances were confronting each other. And as if to confirm what we felt, a second demonstration surged into sight, more disorderly than daring. A band of youths assaulted us with shouts of "Put the loonies in the loony bin!" "*Algérie française!*" (Algeria is French!)

Monsieur Papon made short work of them. He put us all into one basket, shook us up together in the same "*panier à salade,*" the name popularly given to a police van, and served us all up at the same police station. The nonviolent demonstrators were just as calm and relaxed as if they had been at home, but the other young men were outraged. They made a lot of fuss and argued with the police. "But we're *against* them! We're on *your* side! You're making a mistake!"

In short, a poor show.

The very success of this demonstration made it clear to Jo Pyronnet that he must not lead other demonstrations for a long time.

No one, apart from the volunteers, had given a thought to the camps or the suffering of their fellowmen. Conscientious considerations had been swept aside by politics and polemics.

In any case, the volunteers were now merely marking time in a blind alley. And, it must be admitted, they were tired out. It was obvious that, whatever they did, they would never succeed in getting themselves interned. Anyone else who had done a tenth of what they had done would have been behind prison bars. It was clear that prison, like other misfortunes, is for those who flee it, but sometimes those who face it are spared.

A BISHOP SPEAKS HIS MIND

In *La Semaine Religieuse de Lyon* Lord Bishop Ancel published some reflections on the subject of nonviolence:

Not only have we no right to criticize a layman who undertakes [nonviolent] action, but we must recognize that the aim of such action is praiseworthy, since it is to get rid of an injustice. It should also be recognized that nonviolent means are not only permissible but, of all the means employed against injustice, they are certainly the most in conformity with the Gospel.

FAST AND VIGIL IN "BIDONVILLE"[6]
Summer 1960

Our action against the camps, as you have seen, was at a standstill. It was not a failure, since the little band of nonviolent re-

[6] Hovels on the wasteland around a city; a shantytown.

sisters had gained a great deal of experience, strength, and
prestige, but this was not an end in itself. When a wrestler
catches hold of a piece of his opponent's clothing and is left
with it in his hand, there is no point in wrestling with the rag.
We now had to return to the attack from another angle. The
Algerians shut up in camps were not the only victims of arbitrary
treatment, nor are they the most unfortunate. Those who are at
liberty, working or unemployed, live in perpetual expectation of
arrest, of being picked up, searched, and having their papers
checked. Their papers: an identity card and a pay check. The
jobless have no pay check, and consequently merit internment;
a man detained by the police cannot go to work and loses his
job and the pay with which he provides for his family and, as
is often the case, several jobless friends as well. Since the
volunteers had been obstinately refused arrest at the gates of the
camps and by the Ministry of Home Affairs, there was nothing
left for them to do but install themselves among the Algerians
and, as often as one of the latter was pursued or arrested, rush
up and take his place if he fled or be at his side if he
were taken. This new action would have the advantage over
the previous one of making the volunteers more closely acquainted with those they were defending, for till now they
had never seen their faces nor shared their fate other than in
intention.

They chose the *bidonville* at Nanterre, one of the worst
in the Parisian area, where Friends of the Ark had already
begun social work.

There are three parallel asphalt roads running through it.
The area between them is crammed with huts made of planks,
galvanized iron, pieces of tarpaulin, or tarred cardboard. Wind
and rain do great damage, so do the nightly rounds of the
police who, just to make their presence felt, kick down a shaky
door or tear off a bit of roof or stick a hook through a "wall"
or rip it open with pliers.

The volunteers, whose number had now shrunk to nineteen (the others had come to the end of their two months' engagement with us and had returned to their families and their work), set up their quarters with the kind fathers at Petit Colombes, who put the parish hall at their disposal. There, among the props of the small theater, community life took shape—they took turns at washing the dishes and sweeping the floor, had their meals together, listened to readings and talks, observed silence, and in the evening, had prayers around the fire as at the Ark. From the very first days, teams went around prospecting, cleaning, and repairing the damage of the night before; they talked to the Africans and opened a non-paying evening school. Some Africans came, but only a few; the children drew near, but the grown-ups looked on from a distance. We could feel their reticence, could feel them wondering, who are these people? Police in disguise? Missionaries with something up their sleeves? Or people sent by the government?

Meanwhile, the newspapers were announcing a new series of outrages in the capital by the Algerian Liberation Front. The volunteers felt that the time had come to protest against these senseless crimes and that they had acquired the right to do so now that they had put themselves at the service of the Algerian community and were living among them. They prepared to fast for a week, and made this announcement: "We condemn all violence. These criminal acts discredit the cause of Algeria as much as administrative internment discredits the cause of the French government. We beg all Algerians to make their brothers reflect on the obvious fact that bloodshed leads to bloodshed . . . A man like Gandhi can set a people free and furthermore reveal to the whole world the force of nonviolence."

This fast had to be undertaken in the heart of the *bidon-ville*, a quarter of an hour's walk from the over-comfortable parish hall. They began by clearing away a heap of rubbish in order to prepare the ground.

While they were doing so, they had a visit from the police. (It was not the first.)

"Where do you live?"

"Here," they said, pointing to the heap of rubbish.

"No fixed abode, eh? We must arrest you for vagrancy."

"We've been asking you to for two months now."

The police requested orders by radio and were told, "Nonviolent? Don't arrest them on any account! Smash their faces in."

"Do then," said the volunteers as they went on digging.

The cops did not hit them but could not make up their minds to leave them alone, and, out of habit, tried to find some way of catching them out.

"What are you doing?"

"What you see."

"This isn't your place, you have no right to . . ."

"Everybody has the right to work for everybody."

This answer won over one of the questioners.

"That's true!" And, spotting an Algerian who was watching them with his hands in his pockets, "Yes, you there! Why don't you take a spade and come and help them, you lazy b——."

"What about yourself?" said one of our men. "You can take a spade, too, you know."

On the waste ground still stinking from the filth and dead animals we had removed, as well as from the smoke from a nearby chemical factory, the first day of the fast went by clear and calm.

The sky clouded over in the evening and shortly afterward, it began to rain.

The nonviolent had not put a tent up, lest they give the police cause for arresting them, since they now wanted to remain at liberty, at least till the end of their fast. To the fatigue of fasting was added that of no sleep, plus cold and rain. Toward midnight, they sought shelter under the rickety awnings of two small cafés and a grocery, until the bleak morning broke. But a happy surprise was in store for them: as soon as people came out of their huts and the shops opened their shutters, they were surrounded; tongues were loosened, hands outstretched, the last doubts had melted during the night.

"Now we know that you are our brothers!"

"When *we* give our friendship, it is forever," said the Algerians.

The second day, we pitched a tent. Never mind the consequences!

The reporters, who had lost track of the volunteers, were on to them once more. Certain newspaper columns were still filled with polemics about nonviolence and the volunteers, who were not so popular now that their business was no longer in the streets of the capital and now that they had withdrawn into that other continent, Africa of the wasteland. Their silent, purely human work there gave political passion less to feed on.

In the evening, a tall, lean old man wrapped in his jellaba and turban, entered the ring of prayer around the fire. The barriers were down.

Since they had withdrawn among the Algerians and taken to fasting in protest against Algerian atrocities, the volunteers were no longer of great interest either to the right wing or the left. But one fine day a scandal burst into the news as if to tear them out of semi-oblivion.

In every newspaper there was an official declaration by the prefecture of police to the effect that a schoolboy had been arrested, "an active member of Nonviolent Civic Action, carry ing a suitcase containing thirty million francs intended for the support of the rebels, with a list of persons to be done away with." In short, nonviolence had at last been unmasked—the good apostles had bloody knives under their cloaks and machine

guns with which to shoot people in the back. It was an easy
theme to embroider on, and some let themselves go ecstatically.
Most, however, it must be said, accompanied this bit of news
with our official denial or some rather incredulous commentary
of their own. Reporters once again came in flocks, and even the
national radio recorded a statement by the fasters which was
broadcast on the Parisian networks at midday.

The authors of this story did not even take the trouble to
pretend to believe it, and even though the accusation was public,
precise, and serious, it gave rise to not the slightest investigation
at the headquarters of "Action Civique."

The Algerians cluster around the fasting men. Jo speaks to them
of the strength and the resources of nonviolence. Hamdani
translates in a state of exaltation. The audience listens intently,
each man withdrawn into himself.

The little girls like the songs and hymns of the Ark and try
to learn them.

One of them goes toward the fasters, licking an ice cream.
Her sister tugs at her arm: "No, not in front of them!"

Friendship requires giving—but what can one give to fasters?
A group of men has hit on it: a case of bottles of mineral water!
"Like inviting them to tea."

This morning, the volunteers received a letter which threw them
into consternation:

> Your action, good in the beginning, can only discredit us
> now in the eyes of the French nation. Cease all activity, other-
> wise you will see what a good counselor violence well-em-
> ployed can be.

> Signature: [*illegible*]
> Chief of Villaya no. 1.
> [*green rubber stamp*]

Jo goes to the café and spots somebody who looks as if he might well be acquainted with such people. He shows him the bit of paper. "No, it can't be authentic. There's something missing." The signature and the rubber stamp raise some doubts. He'll check.

It turns out to be a fake. But so well done that it can only come from special services well equipped with models for the text. It is not difficult to guess which.

A police van stops two or three times a day near the tent. Sometimes a superintendent gets out, walks up to the group and enters the discussion, in quite a friendly way.

On the sixth day, the attack took place, or rather, the sixth night, a beautiful night with a full moon.

The canvas crashed down like a net on top of the sleepers. Then it was torn away by those who had cut the ropes and were groping for their prey. Their breathing could be heard before their faces were seen.

Who were they? Police? That was not the worst of our men's fears. What they dreaded was that the Algerians should suddenly turn against them.

Now they were in the open, the moonlight as clear as day, God be praised! It was some well-dressed young Frenchmen. They even recognized them—as those who had led a counter-attack against the nonviolent demonstration on the Champs-Élysées.

Everything went off very well under the high moon and in the deep silence, with the lucidity and detachment that come from fasting.

They felt themselves spectators rather than victims of the nocturnal ceremony.

Not a blow, not a cry on one side or the other.

First their sleeping bags were pulled off and then their

clothes. Their hands were tied and they were dragged onto the road.

The power of nonviolence showed plainly in the distance between their own tranquillity and the anxious excitement of their aggressors.

Poor boys, they were visibly disappointed and completely taken aback by this turn of events.

They had had such fun in their schoolboy imaginations, looking forward to this huge practical joke and the roars of laughter that would accompany the telling of it next day. "We took their pants off! Ha-ha! Hee-hee! *Took their pants off!*"

But they had not reckoned with such a moon! nor with these men naked in front of them, lips closed, eyes open.

They did not even try to laugh but attempted in vain to shake off the spell which had turned them into puppets. They ran away, taking the clothes with them.

But the men they had left naked on the road followed them.

And when the fugitives looked around, like a murderer pursued by the ghost of his victim, they fled with smothered cries and rushed to their cars.

The Colombes priests, who had somehow or other learned what had happened, arrived quickly with clothes and blankets and then left them. The fasters lay sleepless on the flattened canvas of their tent, till dawn, which was the dawn of the seventh day.

Evening of the seventh day. The feast of the breaking of the fast.

The Companion Mary and Parisian Friends of the Ark arrived with baskets and parcels, set up a table on the wasteland, decorated it with greenery and loaded it with fruit, dairy products, and cakes. The neighborhood Algerians brought

bananas, doughnuts, curds, and orangeade. Priests and parishioners came from Colombes. Standing around the table, they
all watched the volunteers eat. The food was so plentiful that
everyone shared it.

They went and took up their quarters again in the parish
hall at Colombes. Three teams now took shifts to ensure a constant presence in the *bidonville.*

They made a point of being there when police cars stopped
so as to follow the men on their rounds, to be present at their
lockpicking and searches, to stand there silent when they tipped
beds over, emptied drawers onto the ground in front of terrified
children, manhandled fathers and dragged them away, and lined
up men to search them. Then the volunteers would step into the
line too and raise their arms, so as to undergo search and arrest.
They would climb into the Black Marias and sit on the benches
beside the Algerians and get down only when forced to.

There were several commissariats and gendarmeries making
raids every night. They didn't seem to know about each other.
Whoever complained of the previous night's ill treatment was
told that it had nothing to do with the policeman he was talking
to. It was always the others who had done the damage. In any
case, there were few complaints.

"Look here, it's the third time you've arrested this man to
check his identity. Surely you're beginning to know who he is?"

The worthy cop's answer was, "That's what they need to keep
them in hand."

"Do you think you're managing to?"

A new police patrol meets the patrolling volunteers.

"What are you doing here?"

"Keeping an eye on things."

"What things?"

"The police."

"That's enough of that. Clear off. Get moving!"
They moved—in the same direction as the police.

It was on night patrol that they witnessed the worst scenes, and
no doubt their mere presence had a moderating effect. For the
forces of order, as they are called, were in the habit of letting
themselves go completely at night. They would burst into quiet
cafés, machine guns pointed, and smash up the bottles, or into
a hovel where some family was asleep, break the dishes, turn
everything upside down, and sack the place on the pretext that
arms were hidden there, and there would be no end to their
search since there were no arms to be found. The silent observa-
tion of the nonviolent and their occasional intervention when
they offered themselves to be hit, as you can imagine, infuriated
the nocturnal bullies.

One of the volunteers spent the night in a hut which measured
about two square yards. Its occupant had invited him in because
there was room for a guest, since, as it was raining, he couldn't
lie down. When it rained, the water trickled down the head
of his bed, so he had to roll the matteress up at that end, and
when it rained harder, water trickled down at the foot of the
bed, so he had to roll it up at that end too. A third stream, a
stream of mud, poured in from the plank forming the entrance-
way. Only the suitcase on four sticks remained dry. That was
what mattered most, for it contained the clean shirt and dry
clothes needed next morning for work at the factory.

Avoiding invitations and gifts without hurting anyone's
feelings requires great care and sometimes cunning. But sometimes cunning is on the other side. Jacques, seated at the corner
of a hut, was singing when suddenly a packet of cigarettes fell
on his knees and the man who was responsible ran off like a
thief.

. . .

Evening classes were still going on, and more and more people came.

As the days went by, the volunteers saw ever more clearly what a need there was for this work of education, hygiene, protection, and reconciliation, and were amazed not to have thought of it sooner. If only it could spread in space and time until it became permanent in all the breeding grounds of wretchedness and revolt. There lay the best field for nonviolent army maneuvers.

But as the month drew to a close, they had to give it up, for the simple reason that they had neither the strength nor the resources to maintain their effort.

No, not give it up, suspend it. Suspend it in order to work out a way of enlarging it and including another category of victims of the war in Algeria.

For the fact was that the people of Algeria were not alone in experiencing its horror. Right behind them, in order of degradation, came the young people of France. Young men just out of school or the seminary, who were forced into it, remained marked forever by the things they saw and did. The biggest victims were those who firmly refused to take part in it, and every day there were more of them.

The nonviolent volunteers, headed by Jo Pyronnet, were ready to support their cause and share their fate.

4

FOR CONSCIENTIOUS OBJECTION AND CIVILIAN SERVICE

THE SEVEN BOISGONTIERS
AND THE PÉRIGORDIAN

September 1960

At the beginning of September a meeting took place between the leaders of Civic Action and supporters from other associations for the purpose of drawing up texts and plans.

The persons thus exposing themselves to legal punishment fell into one of three categories:

1. Young men
2. The co-signatories of Jo Pyronnet's letter to the President of the Republic
3. Volunteers campaigning for conscientious objection and civilian service

1. The young men were soldiers who were going to walk out and tell their officers where to find them at work, or students who had refused deferment, or boys already drafted and waiting for their papers.

The young people wrote a letter to the President asking for permission to perform some kind of civilian service in Algeria. Two dangers threatened them: first, that of finding themselves between the devil and the deep blue sea, or between the army and the rebels, which would have made work, and even life, impossible to anyone who refused to serve one side at the expense of the other.

Also, in spite of their intention to work on the spot for the sole good of the population, they ran a second risk, that of bringing grist to the mill of colonial propaganda and serving as a psychological weapon. (In view of the immense difficulties involved, what would most probably happen was also most to be desired, namely, that the government would reject their proposal and put them under them lock and key.)

The young men took it upon themselves to let others of their age know about their project and to rally support. There were five of them to begin with.

2. In general, the co-signatories were older men, over draft age, who backed up the actions of the young people. For this reason, they signed Jo Pyronnet's letter to the President of the Republic, supporting and explaining the young people's request. They also signed the Appeal to Young Men which they wanted to see published in the press. But the newspapers did not dare to publish it and it was distributed in the mail or by hand. Co-signatories ran the risk of being charged with inciting the military to disobedience, a charge which carried heavy sentences, and therein lay the value of their signature. There were over a hundred signatures at the start, among them, those of priests and Protestant ministers, and the more signatures, of course, the less the danger.

3. The volunteers worked full time for the civilian service campaign, advising and helping the young people. When the latter were arrested, they barred the way, not to prevent their arrest, but in order to be arrested with them. There were ten

volunteers, most of whom were among the thirty of the previous campaign.

The assembly at Pasquier in September was far from being as orderly and friendly as the nonviolence camps and gatherings at the Ark. There was a bit of friction between the supporters of "absolute nonviolence" and those of "tactical nonviolence." Here and there, political hatred broke out. Some among the most generous and devoted felt obliged to use vulgar or foul language in order to win popularity. Sometimes I wonder which are the most difficult to love: our enemies or our friends!

This wrangling was only a foretaste of much more serious internal conflict which almost wrecked the action at the outset.

One of the young people who had asked Jo to help a student, Alain, called for a meeting of volunteers so as to "come to an agreement on what they would answer the police if they were questioned." "Just tell the truth," said Jo. But Alain would not hear of it and wanted to work out a clever scheme. The conclusion forced on the volunteers was that this young man's place was not in a Satyagraha. After days and nights of discussion, they resolved to separate from him. He won over another young man to his ideas as well as a number of our supporters in press and government circles, then took the place the thirty had prepared in the Nanterre *bidonville.*

So the volunteers went to Terrasson, a rural parish which had been flooded and laid waste by the Dordogne. They took with them the three remaining young men: Pierre Boisgontier who had quit his barracks leaving his address behind, Jack Muir who had his papers, and Jean-Pierre Hémon, who was about to be drafted, and was the first of the children raised in the Ark to have become eligible for military service.

The mayor installed them in the youth hostel. Jojo, the fat cook, made soup and tarts for them. The farmers whose corn crop they were coming to save welcomed them with gratitude and astonishment, "for people don't often think of us country folk."

When the gendarme came to fetch "Boisgontier Pierre," he found three of him, each affirming that he was Pierre Boisgontier.

"Which of the three of you is Pierre Boisgontier? Come on, out with it!"

"I'm telling you," they each repeated, "it's me."

"If you go on pulling my leg, it'll be the worse for you!"

It did get worse. Four others arrived, each of them affirming, "It's me."

"Show me your papers!" shouted the gendarme.

"We have nothing to show!"

He became threatening, "I'll take the whole lot of you!"

"Do," they said.

The poor man didn't know whether to get angry or laugh. It was a crazy business. Laughter got the better of him. "I'll take all of you. You can sort it out with the captain" (of the rural constables).

As he led them off to the gendarmerie, he was assailed by the remarks of the country people. "It's not often decent people come and help us, and there you go taking them away! Surely you're not going to make out that they're criminals! You're not going to do them any harm, are you?"

"It's nothing serious, just an identity check. It'll be all right."

But the morning wasn't long enough. Faced with such an unprecedented situation, the captain exhausted himself repeating questions that got him nowhere. Then he plunged into a study of legal rules and regulations, consulted a tribunal and returned to the telephone in order to speak to the barracks.

"Hallo? Hallo! We have arrested Boisgontier Pierre . . .

Yes, sir . . . Very well, sir . . . But the trouble is there are seven of them . . . Yes, seven . . . Three and four . . . But we can't find out . . . Yes, yes . . . No . . . Oh? You're sending somebody to identify him? Very well, sir. Over."

It was past midday. The gendarmes had come back from their rounds and there were a number of them. This was the moment Jo chose to make the discussion general. He stood up, spoke of nonviolence, the actions at Thol, Vincennes, and Nanterre, the war in Algeria, young people, and what the presence of the volunteers meant.

Never had he spoken to a more attentive audience. The gendarmes stood listening eagerly, nodding, and rolling their eyes.

Jojo was summoned and came with his steaming dishes. The captain jumped at this opportunity to interrogate him. Jojo was under legal obligation to enter his guests' names and addresses on his register. Had he done so? "But the volunteers are not my guests," said Jojo. "They were invited by the parish. It's none of my business." He didn't know which of all these Boisgontiers was the right one. He acted the fool with great subtlety, although the volunteers had not tipped him off.

A gendarme insisted on laying the table with a tablecloth. It was late and he had not eaten because of all this unusual activity. "It doesn't matter," he said. "It'll do me good to fast a little too."

The solution came toward evening.

The captain had found out some time previously which was the real Boisgontier, but he had no legal proof or legal means of procuring any. And all at once, the correct phrase flashed into his mind.

"The fact is that you refuse to show your papers! It's a legal offense! Offense number one!

"The fact is that at least six of you have declared a false identity. It's a legal offense! The second one!

"The fact is, you are trying to mislead the authorities in their investigation. It's an offense, so you will have to be arrested and searched!"

This time they were forcibly separated, and the innocent six were released.

They went back to the hostel and conferred.

Boisgontier would probably be taken back to Mourmelon by train, so they must go and look for him at the station.

They went in vain to Terrasson and saw the last train leave.

There remained a slight hope of finding him on the night train at Brive station.

They went there and lay down in the waiting room while Cécile and Jean kept a look-out.

Toward midnight they were roused by a shout. "He's there— platform three."

They stayed hidden in the underground passage until the train arrived from Paris. Jean, whom the gendarmes didn't know, stood conspicuously at the head of the staircase. At his signal, they rushed on to the platform, encircling the prisoner and his gendarmes.

Helpless with surprise, shouting and gesticulating, the gendarmes yelled to some soldiers to come to their aid, furious to find them so lukewarm and to see that the civilians were rushing away.

Turning on their prisoner, they tried to push him toward the train, but Jean-Pierre, crawling between their legs, threw his arms around Boisgontier's knees and held him tight.

Unable to move, he fell with the volunteers on top of him in a pile. The gendarmes kicked and punched the heap.

The train pulled out without further ado. Police reinforcements arrived in a new explosion of rage.

While Boisgontier was being handcuffed, Jo Pyronnet shot

out his arm and the second manacle was snapped on to his wrist.

The two friends exchanged a long look. They were linked by the chain.

They located their gendarme again, but found him beside himself. "Imagine doing that to me! And to think I served them on a tablecloth! They got round me, the swine! They took advantage of my kindness! But they won't catch me out again, or I'm not a Périgordian!"

They appeared before the magistrate next day, charged with resisting arrest, assaulting and wounding public officials, and attempting to aid and abet a deserter to escape from the hands of the law.

They pointed out that, although the nonviolent are in the habit of pleading guilty, they had intended not to enable Boisgontier to escape from justice but, on the contrary, to submit to that justice themselves; that Boisgontier was not a deserter since he had informed his seniors of his departure and the reasons for it, and had left his address, that it was they, the accused, who had undergone assault and battery.

"Yes, yes," the magistrate agreed, "the gendarmes themselves testify to all that. We'll see about it at the trial."

"And when can we expect the trial?"

"Oh, later, later on. Maybe never."

They were free, all except Boisgontier, free to continue since they had not yet done enough to justify imprisonment.

THE TRIAL

November 1961

If I had undertaken to write a play entitled "The Pyronnet Affair," with a view to explaining the doctrine of nonviolence in as popular and moving a manner as possible, using all the resources of dramatic art, contriving the effects, the surprises, the reversals, and inventing an original character with a background and history to illustrate each aspect of the problem, I could certainly never have composed anything so good as the great impromptu show which took place in the law court at Carpentras on November 22, 1961.

That day, I was in Tierra del Fuego, on the far side of the other hemisphere. I pictured the provincial judge at grips with the case, unforeseen and without precedent in French law. I put into his mouth some burlesque and not very funny remarks and replies which were scarcely suited to the tragic and grandiose decor of the Antarctic sky, and even less to the anxiety I felt at being so far away from my men on the day of their ordeal. Once more, I must acknowledge that what really happened was more incredible than anything I could conjure up.

The crowd in the courtroom, which was a fairly small one, was tightly packed and overflowed into the corridors. The benches were so placed that the judicial assembly was closely surrounded by the public, who were so jammed in and listened so intently that, although silent, there was no doubt they played an important part in the trial.

The presiding magistrate had a reputation for dealing with things quickly. From the start he did his best to live up to his reputation. Without preamble, he fired questions at the accused, cutting their answers short, and hurried through the reports of the police and the plaintiffs, not because of negligence nor for lack of consideration for the accused, far from it, but so as to get straight to the point. "You are nonviolent, therefore truthful and courageous. You are not men to resort to sidetracking or pettifogging, you therefore acknowledge that you committed the acts imputed to you, which simplifies my task." For this judge, the case was obviously judged beforehand. Jo tried several times to interrupt him and get a hearing, but was himself interrupted. The dialogue became hurried, disjointed, then faltered, then marked time and began to go round in circles.

"But at least you *do* acknowledge the facts?" shouted the judge.

Jo: "What facts?"

The judge: "Those you are charged with, inciting the military to disobedience!"

Jo: "No, not at all."

The judge: "Your appeal to young people contains the words, 'If civilian service is refused to you by the authorities, accept imprisonment rather than carry arms.' If that isn't incitement and provocation, what is it?"

Jo: "An appeal to conscience."

The judge: "An appeal so worded raises doubts in the minds of simple boys who have hitherto asked themselves no questions, and for those who have some hesitation, it is a pressure toward refusal; it is therefore just what the law means by 'incitement.'"

Jo: "Incitement involves moral pressure on those who are hesitant, but all that is contrary to nonviolence. I would avoid pressuring anybody to do anything and I would be careful not to encourage, or even accept, anyone who had any hesitation."

An argument then broke out about the word "incitement," in which each accused the other of playing on words. Just as they were reaching a deadlock, the lawyer intervened and asked (not without relevancy) that the witnesses should be heard. It was up to them to say whether they had made up their own minds or whether they had been forced or seduced.

It was like a breath of fresh air. Immediately, everything became clear, simple, and human.

The first witnesses called on were three young offenders who had been brought out of prison and made to travel handcuffed.

Their evidence was sober. Their words, their tone, and their silences were firm and strong. Strong because it was prison which had come into the dock and was speaking. Prison is another world. And when a man has gone to prison deliberately, for the sake of justice, his evidence rings true in a way no eloquence can match.

There were eleven other young men in the same situation. They had not been brought. But these three represented the three degrees of conscience and resistance to which nonviolence has given shape and expression.

The first had been a soldier for eleven months. It was not service in the army or wearing uniform that he objected to, but rather (independently of any sect or party) the war in Algeria and its atrocities. That was why, one day when he was on leave, he went to work on a building site instead of returning to the barracks.

The second was a conscientious objector who, the day he was drafted, championed resistance with as much fervor as a soldier going off to war. He had rallied Nonviolent Civic Action by letter and had been supported and his cause taken up by the nonviolent[1] along with that of Henri Cheyrouze, who was already in prison and famous for his hunger strikes when our campaign began.

The third was an anarchist and deserter who, for the purposes of the campaign, had come back from abroad.[2]

All stated that for them the choice was not between obedience and disobedience, but between the various forms of disobedience open to them. These were: to desert, which would not be testifying; to rebel, which is contrary to love of one's country, even if one judges that country severely; to become a conscientious

---

[1] The action at Aix for René Nazon.

[2] André Bernard, who gave himself up for arrest, chained to six volunteers, in Marseilles in May 1961.

objector of the traditional kind, a way of testifying which requires great honesty and great courage, but to which one goes
alone and beaten beforehand; or, lastly, nonviolent civic action,
which is the same testimony, but collective and organized, social
and constructive, and a sure solution to the painful immediate
problem.

They asserted that they had been neither pushed nor pressured
but, on the contrary, were warned of the dangers and ordeals to
which they were exposing themselves, and were urged not to
make a hasty decision, but to reflect on all aspects of the problem first.

At this point, Jean-Marie Domenach, editor of the review
Esprit, rose, pale, and, in a voice choking with emotion, said:
"You ask me, Monsieur le Président, to testify to the morality
of the accused. How can I deliver certificates of morality about
men whose example I have not the spiritual strength to follow?
Bernanos says that what redeems a nation from the disgrace of
tyranny is a certain proportion of free men. I look on the
accused as free men."

Then came Hamdani, the young Moslem.

"I am Algerian, twenty-nine years old. I am different from
those who have appeared here in handcuffs as deserters from
the French army. Thanks to the Ark and Jo Pyronnet, I am a
defaulter from the National Liberation Front, although I remain in agreement with its aims. What impressed me, convinced
me and won me over to the nonviolent was to see for the first
time men, Frenchmen, whose way of loving their country was to
want it to be innocent of crime and irreproachable; men who,
whether dealing with enemies or friends, whether for a good
cause or a bad, refuse to resort to bloodshed, plotting, lying and
propaganda, and legal or illegal manslaughter.

"When I saw them protesting against the internment camps

in which my fellow countrymen are arbitrarily imprisoned, and insisting that they should be imprisoned in their stead or with them, I couldn't help joining their campaign.

"As their present action in favor of conscientious objectors did not concern me so directly, I asked to withdraw in order to reflect; also in order to contact old friends and teach them nonviolence, for I know that nonviolence could set my unhappy country free as it set India free under the leadership of Gandhi.

"But I could not find a way of convincing them or touching their hearts.

"So now I want to rejoin the rank of the nonviolent, for there I am sure of serving both countries and preparing peace and reconciliation. In the meantime, I am learning to free myself from myself."

Claude Voron, aged twenty-three, is a student of astronomy training at the National Center of Scientific Research, whose draft had been deferred. The quick, birdlike movements of his head, his clear voice with its cheerful southern lilt dispelled some of the gravity of the preceding statements.

"I have been taking part in the action for eight months, going from one place to another. I am a rebel against military service and a volunteer for civilian service. I refused deferment and sent my papers back and am now at the disposal of the law," he stated.

The judge: "You seem quite satisfied with this arrangement, but I'm not sure that the law is satisfied. And now, young man, if you are a rebel, how is it that you are free?"

Claude Voron: "I wonder myself. On the twenty-eighth of October, I went to the gendarmerie. They said, 'Since you are nonviolent, wait till you're sent for, be patient.' And they turned me out!" (Laughter in court.)

The judge: "Is it to Civic Action that you owe inspiration for your refusal?"

Claude Voron: "I found it all by myself, but they inspired me with the right way of going about it. Some people said to me, 'Better to do two years of service than five in prison' and others, 'Why don't you go abroad rather than undergo two years of service and perhaps war too.' Everybody has his own way of getting round the law. Only the nonviolent said to me, 'Accept responsibility for your act: go to the gendarmes, we'll go with you.' "

Now Pastor Trocmé lifts his majestic bulk, his noble, pensive head. Profound conviction makes his voice quiver.

"It may seem surprising that a Protestant minister should give evidence in favor of Marie Faugeron and Jo Pyronnet, who are both fervent Catholics. But I am not the only one: the Protestant ministers Vernier and Lerch, Lasserre and Blanchet have put their signatures to the appeal as well as I. Indeed, I can't help wondering why, if these men are accused, we are not! I am a witness that the act of which they are accused by the justice of men is solely motivated by their fidelity to Christ, who is their master and mine. It is in order to follow His 'new commandment' that they have left their families and their employment, their comfort and convenience to put themselves at the service of the poorest, and have invited young people to do the same instead of shedding blood.

"If they are guilty because they claim the right not to kill, and want civil instead of military service, then we are guilty too and have even preceded them by several decades.

"The civilian service they are asking for has already been instituted in Holland, England, the United States, Sweden, Norway, Denmark, Canada, and Germany.

"In France, the head of state has already promised it. In a few months, God willing, peace may have returned and the statute of conscientious objectors granted at last. Today's accused will then be looked on as forerunners and prophets.

"We beg the honor of being associated with them. We want justice to be done, to them and to us, in the highest sense of the term."

The afternoon session opened with the statement of Father Cortade, a Dominican.

"Yes, I do swear to tell the whole truth, for, as a priest, I am vowed to it, vowed to serve it in a very concrete fashion among the people I meet with.

"Like so many other priests, I have been led by my ministry to witness the tragic conflict caused by the Algerian war in the consciences of young people. I am a witness of their rejection of this war, not out of fear of fighting or of taking risks, but out of fear of serving the wrong cause and being ordered to commit terrible acts. I am a witness of the torment their refusal can lead to. And I am a witness of the more serious spiritual damage sometimes brought about by their reluctant submission and a few months of compulsory service in Africa. I know to what degradation and despair some have been reduced. I have seen young men returning from Algeria as from a horrible illness or the loss of reason.

"The way my friends, the accused, have opened up and courageously taken to support those who follow it, avoids this alternative. I shall not try to show that it is not contrary to the law. Nevertheless, I think it is morally legitimate. I read somewhere in the Gospel that it is better to obey God than men, and my old master St. Thomas teaches that conscience always compels, for God speaks with the voice of conscience and disobedience to one's conscience is sin.

"There was no incitement to disobedience but a fraternal

welcome to consciences, so as to demonstrate the truth and give them the strength to act accordingly."

There was other evidence, some of it more or less muddled, and some of it fine, but as I have only had vague accounts of it, I shall not dwell on it.

Every time a witness ventured a remark like: ". . . because of the loathing I felt at the idea of taking part in an unjust war . . ." the judge shouted, "Stop! Stick to the point! We don't require evidence of your opinions, but evidence of the influence of the accused on your decision," or again, "We want evidence concerning the morality of the accused, and nothing else."

At last it was Pierre Boisgontier's turn. His case, as you remember, had opened the campaign.

Our friend has a harelip, which complicates his diction and peppers his speech with little squeaks, but he has a ready tongue for all that, and is as bold in word as in deed. When he told the court that, after eight months of imprisonment, he had been freed because of "sinusitis," everybody burst out laughing.

"You would perhaps like me to say that I have been incited or pressured by the accused. Well, I must tell you that I'm the one who used the incitement, the pressuring too, for as soon as I could get a hold of Jo, I pressed and insisted for all I was worth. It wasn't an easy job, he's a difficult customer. *He* was in no hurry. He had other things to do, he already had the business of the internment camps on his hands. 'Aren't you going to do anything for us?' I would say, 'You're going to do what they all do. They say they want peace in Algeria and then do nothing! And then they let us young people go off to Africa but they take good care not to go themselves!'

"Civilian service in Algeria, for the reconciliation of the two nations, is *my* idea, and as it's a very good idea, I didn't want to keep it all to myself, so I spoke to the Students' Union about it, also to Young Resistance and the underground network, and what they said was, 'The government can't possibly accept that. You'll get five years' imprisonment, and it will all be for nothing. *We* don't ask for anything, we just get the hell out of it!' I spoke to several members of parliament and senators and journalists who said to me, 'Very good idea! Come and see me again. I'm very interested.'

"I waited and waited, counting socks in the commissary, disgusted with doing nothing in a safe place, and in a parachutist's uniform at that.

"But as soon as I read in the newspapers about the nonviolent and above all about their big chief, I knew he was the man we needed to lead us. So I never left him alone, prodding and egging him on till one day he said, 'Since you are leaving the army in any case, and since your peace project is sound and I believe in it, all right, we'll help you.'

"And shortly afterward, he added another idea to mine. 'Since you will be prevented from doing civilian service in Algeria, instead of asking for it in the abstract, let us actually create it in France, starting tomorrow. Let's open work sites and do our demonstrations with picks and shovels and barrows in our hands.' "

When Boisgontier had finished his story and spoken of the help he had received from the nonviolent while in prison and how he had gone to them as soon as he had been released, he left the witness stand. Then, turning suddenly, he came back and said, "I forgot to say that I am their accomplice."

The judge broke in, "For there to be complicity, there must be an offense, but that has not been established."

It was obvious that the wind had turned.

Right from the beginning, and throughout the trial, the judge had shown his esteem for the accused, and his respect for objectivity. But, being quick-witted and intelligent, and having studied the written evidence and drawn support from letters and telegrams from all over the world, he had immediately grasped the situation; that is, he had seen precisely how this many-sided personal and national drama (which he had no intention of fathoming) could be put into a simple legal formula that would satisfy the conscience of honest civil servants, cut short their scruples, and in itself bear full responsibility for the verdict.

He planned to take from the statements, and from the evidence of the accused and the witnesses, the hard facts that would support his opinion. As soon as an unexpected aspect of the problem cropped up, he treated it as a digression or a delay, an obstacle which he did his best to overcome, and whenever a witness was shy or muddled or lacked conviction, he tied him up in knots.

But now he was visibly absorbed and upset. He was listening and reflecting.

Jo was able to get a word in again and point out, with his characteristic force of persuasion, the essential features of the discussion.

"I think it has been sufficiently proved by the copious evidence from witness after witness that we have neither incited nor provoked anyone, much less applied pressure or force. But that is not enough. It must also be stated that I myself have been forced to devote my attention to young people driven to distraction by the war in Algeria. I have been forced, not so much by their insistence or their anxious longing for help, as by the very logic of nonviolence.

"I say *forced* because I confess that I should have preferred to persuade myself that it could not be done, or that there was nothing to be done, or that, after all, it was none of my business.

"For I had weighed the difficulties and dangers of the undertaking. The worst of these was doubtless that we might be too successful, that we might be efficient beyond all our expectations and that the results might get out of hand, that we might be compromised by allies we had not chosen, that side issues and counter-shocks, and division, confusion, and disorder might ensue, in a word, that the contrary of what we wanted might happen.

"These risks existed and still exist, but we had to take them and just do our best to ward them off day by day, for not to take them was to run the even greater risk of doing nothing and so missing our vocation of nonviolent men conspicuous for speaking and acting in the name of conscience. Had we not acted, we should in the end have been accountable to the young men who, subjected to all kinds of pressure and incitement, threats and constraint, pose for their elders an urgent and vital question. We should have been accountable to them because, knowing the answer, we had refused to give it, and the answer is this: 'Obey your conscience.' The answer is also that we should allow them to do so, and commit ourselves along with them.

"People speak to these young men, and, as was to be expected, of us as being insubordinate, and seem to imply that everything boils down to whether or not they are willing to wear uniform. But they are so quick to reach that conclusion because they don't consider two things without which it is impossible to form an accurate opinion. In the first place, they do not see the heart of the problem, and then they shut their eyes to the hard facts.

"For, after all, in order to obey nowadays it is not enough to put on a soldier's uniform, one must also know whom one is obeying. You will say 'one's immediate superior.' But if he disobeys his superiors, whom is the soldier to obey? (Nobody will, I think, criticize me for posing a purely hypothetical question.)[3]

---

[3] A sardonic reference to the mutinies that marked the Algerian war.

"And now, quite frankly, supposing this war, which the head of state himself describes as 'fratricidal' and 'absurd,' supposing the whole Algerian affair, in both its means and its ends, were a flagrant breach of the most fundamental laws of respect for mankind and the welfare of nations? You will stop me here, as you have stopped the other witnesses. But the fact remains that, whether one is in the army or not, nowadays it is impossible just to obey without choice, and a man can be judged only on the merits of his chosen loyalty.

" 'Render unto Caesar that which is Caesar's and unto God that which is God's.' In our action I tried to reconcile these two requirements. I don't consider that authority necessarily belongs to Caesar or to the ruler of this world. I believe, like St. Paul, that it may be 'of God.' You can tell by this sign: it carries the arms of God, which are justice and love of the common good. Again like St. Paul, I believe that obedience is a virtue and that we must obey the law 'not only out of fear of punishment, but also for our consciences' sake.' I believe (although the Gospel says nothing about it) that national community is a good thing. We didn't choose it, but we cannot choose that it should be otherwise, nor undo the fact that we have benefited by it, and have a debt of gratitude and honor toward it.

"That is why our appeal insists, 'Do not desert: do nothing that might pass for treason'—advice which displeased some of our friends a great deal and estranged them from us. It is also the reason for our consistently refusing to have anything to do with the underground movement, or to use such slogans as 'The same ends, but different means,' so essential is it for nonviolent resistance that the ends and the means should be of the same nature. Now it is precisely because we support our country and don't want to be separated from it, and because we respect lawful authority and the persons of our rulers and have not the slightest desire to get rid of them, and still less, to take their place, that we feel the errors and crimes being committed in the name of France to be evils for which we are responsible; we do not judge or denounce, so much as confess them. Our action is aimed at them, but still more, by the tribulation into which it leads us, to atone for them.

"And now, let us return to the risks of losing sight of the main issue and behaving equivocally. What precautions have we taken against this? Instead of trying to be clever or careful, we have stuck to this maxim: 'Don't sacrifice the tiniest particle of truth to expediency, however tempting it might be.'

"Thus, the plan to open work camps right away in order to help the people was welcomed wholeheartedly by our young men, but we felt that what mattered more than the work itself (although they were not always aware of it) was putting up a show. They wanted to get together, to demonstrate, to arouse public opinion, to attract the attention of the press. As for the work, it was more of a polemical argument to them, a symbolic gesture rather than something to be undertaken and carried out.

"Our first work camp was at Terrasson where we were out of the public eye, far away from Paris and everywhere else. Most of our demonstrations took place in the provinces, but we did more work than we made speeches. When we were arrested, we saw to it that the work sites we had to abandon were taken over by International Civil Service and other less vulnerable organizations.

"This discretion was a great disappointment to some people. Several of them lost heart or left. We ourselves were fairly pleased with the results of so much effort: first of all, with the spiritual progress made by those who took part in the work, for work is the school of the nonviolent. It was a way of preparing them for prison and other trials and of establishing a connection with the population to whom they had given their friendly help. There were also welcome changes of heart among some of the people who attended our demonstrations or visited us in our huts, especially among those whose job it was to oppose us: gendarmes, police, inspectors, jailers, judges, and ministers, not to mention our cellmates in prison.

"What matters above all in a nonviolent action is that it should accord with the truth and that it should be understood.

"That was the very reason for the trial and our defense. Although, contrary to what you expected, Monsieur le Président, we are trying to contest the charges and are pleading not guilty, nobody should think that we are doing so to avoid responsibility or punishment.

"We are doing so in order to explain the particular nature of our action, for we have the right to be punished for what we have done, not to be judged on misunderstandings and vague reports. Now, the very nature of nonviolent action is responsibility and even voluntary co-responsibility.

"This is the moment to speak of one of the charges brought against me: that I sent back my service and conduct record. I did so in protest against the treatment inflicted on one of our men. Contrary to the law of military justice, he had been kept in barracks, then transferred to Algeria, in civilian clothes. But a person who, publicly and in advance, makes known his decision not to submit, must be handed over to military justice: however, in practice, more often than not, he is kept in the army where he may have to undergo all kinds of treatment intended to make him change his mind. Another of our men, one of the witnesses summoned but who has been unable to come, was half strangled in his cell by an officer.

"You call our nonviolent appeal pressure, but what do you call attempting to strangle a man? It is true you have not been asked to judge that question, and that is the whole point. I shall not insist.

"My purpose in returning my army record was to expose myself to punishment by the law so as to show up the illegality of such treatment, and ease the pressure on the consciences of young people.

"These young people are serving long prison sentences, and if we, who have supported them by assuming their identity when they were arrested and demanding to be given the same sentence, were let off after this trial with just a fine or were treated with leniency, it would be a real scandal."

This was followed by the statement of the public prosecutor.

He began by saying that the facts had been proved and the law broken.

He ended with these astonishing words: "I await the decision of the court with confidence. I am convinced that, as far as possible, it will reconcile consideration for the honesty of the accused and the nobility of their motives with the laws by which we are ruled and which are imposed on the legislative assemblies by the urgent requirements of the times in which we live. Let us hope that some day humanity will become aware of its true vocation and progress beyond the questions which have occupied us today."

Maître[4] Gaspari spoke next; he was so overcome with emotion that he spoke with difficulty. He felt that in such cases where neither the accused nor the witnesses hid or feared anything, an attorney was out of place, unless as another witness.

"Words can add nothing to an action which is more eloquent through its many witnesses than anything I could say."

When Maître Bouchet's turn came, everyone felt that, as everything had already been said, his speech would be superfluous.

Yet, after a hearing which had lasted four hours and during which attention had never flagged, he succeeded in holding the

[4] French attorney's title.

attention of the court and the public and kept his audience hanging on his words throughout his lengthy summing-up. Every word of it rang true and was pertinent, clear, and forceful.

"Monsieur le Président, you like people to answer questions with a Yes or a No. I shall try to fulfill that requirement.

"So let us consider whether, yes or no, the aim of the action is wrong. Its aim was to substitute the service of the poor for armed service in order to repair war damage and to prepare for peace through reconciliation.

"To ask the question is to answer it: the aim is highly praiseworthy.

"But perhaps this is Utopian and impractical?

"No, it is reasonable and constructive. So much so that eighteen nations have written it into their law.

"We are not dealing with dreamers. Consider the name of their movement: Civic Action. The words mean what they say.

"In actual fact, these men opened a work site at the same time that they launched their appeal and request.

"But perhaps their proposal is inopportune and premature?

"No. We have been promised that a statute of conscientious objectors will be granted at the end of the Algerian war. In other words, we shall be given the remedy when the disease has done its worst.

" 'Uneasiness among young people.' 'Uneasiness in the army.' These expressions were not invented by the nonviolent. What is the extent of the evil? How many thousands of young Frenchmen have crossed the border to escape a problem they could not solve? We cannot name a figure with certainty, but what do figures matter? Were there only one solitary noble conscience troubled by the impossibility of bringing its moral requirements into agreement with the laws of the state, that conscience would have a right to obtain satisfaction from society.

"Nobody can blame the nonviolent for having sought the answer to this question. The answer our society does not give.

"Nobody will contest that their solution is a way out of the impasse and that it is better, morally better, than all the others of today, including that of total obedience.

"It is clear that the proposed way out excludes all others, including that of blind submission to the law. Is it an illegal way out, then? Or is it not rather a way of achieving progress?

"In a democracy, is opposition contrary to the law? It is a brake, an incentive, a way of correcting power and a guarantee of freedom.

"Waldeck-Rousseau says, 'All moral progress is, to start with, an action undertaken by a minority.' He also says, 'The essential is to be right, the majority is a question of time.'

"Now let us consider the means open to this minority, this tiny minority, this, shall we say, privileged, nonviolent minority.

"We have recognized the value of their ends, can it be that their means, their nonviolent means, are wrong?

"In defense of a holy cause, even violent means seem justified. How could nonviolent means not be?

"Will violence always be the great midwife of history?

"Even great leaders and politicians have, at the end of their careers, come to recognize the failure of their methods. 'There are two forces in the world,' said Napoleon, 'that of the sword, that of the spirit. The force of the spirit will finally always conquer the force of the sword.' And Lyautey, 'Nothing true is ever founded on force.' And Clemenceau, who was not exactly a bleating lamb and had no soft spot for clergymen, 'If Christians had one drop of St. Francis's blood in their veins, the world would be changed.' "

The verdict was postponed for three weeks. It was:

>Joseph Pyronnet—ten months.
>Jacques Tinel (who was responsible for the demonstrations in Paris)—eight months.

Marie Faugeron (Companion of the Ark)—six months.
Simone Pacot (Companion of the Ark)—six months.

All were granted reprieves.

5

THE GREAT
ROME FAST

THE FORTY DAYS

On his arrival in Rome, Shantidas sent this letter to Pope
John XXIII.

Rome, March 4, 1963

Holy Father,

In answer to your appeal,[1] I have come from France to
Rome to do penance for the sake of the Council, the Council
of Reconciliation we have been dreaming of for years without
ever dreaming that it might really take place soon.

I am going to fast until Easter morning and thus offer up
forty days of intense, silent prayer.

There are three reasons for my doing so:

The first is consciousness of the sins that make me unfit
to address my prayer to heaven.

The second is the prayer itself: that our Pope be given
health, for he has won our affection by trying to change pon-
tifical majesty into fatherly kindness.

The third is our hopeful longing, in face of the threat of

---

[1] A reference to the encyclical *"Pœnitentiam Agere."*

total war, for the message of peace the world needs today, the bold, absolute, in short, the evangelical word.

Allow me to dwell at some length on this point of vital importance. Indeed, what will all the good we expect from the Council profit us if the total war being prepared turns us into a pile of corpses or a population of lepers or if, even without war, atomic fallout transforms future generations into freaks?

I know that Your Holiness dislikes prophets of woe and I have no wish to be one. But do not say that all this is only science fiction. It is inscribed in the mad logic of our times. Moreover, the holocaust of the whole earth may be touched off at any moment by mere accident.

Who will protect them from their leaders, the blind leading the blind, themselves led by the Prince of this World?

Who will protect God's creation and all the beauty and goodness it contains against covetousness, fear, and pride already armed to destroy all things?

Who, if not the Church, *"Mater et Magistra"*?

It is up to her to warn, exhort, implore, and show the way out.

See what has happened in Switzerland where an archbishop urged the nation to consent to the instrument of death. If Rome had spoken out, this shame would not lie upon us Catholics. If Rome does not speak out now, this unfortunate example will be followed and the peril increased.

It is true that the Church has no power to impose her will on lawful governments, nor to oppose them, unless she is prepared to return to the catacombs. But the question is not to impose or oppose nor to address governments since governments will go on putting the blame for aggression on the adversary and wait for the other country to disarm first; no one will ever take the first step toward disarmament.

It is a question of refuting the accusation of the enemies

of our Church who say that she is the accomplice of governments in their bloody enterprises and that Papal declarations in favor of peace are only so much theory and rhetoric, perhaps even a front.

The argument is very difficult to contest as long as a misinterpretation of Romans 13 makes a religious duty of blind obedience to established power, however bad it may be.

There is no hope but in God, and God works from within, in the consciences of free men. The only hope is therefore in an awakening of Christian conscience, and its proper education to render it capable of resisting the temptation, seduction, and constraint by which power draws it into its game.

Spiritual resistance is quite the contrary of rebellion, subversion, and anarchy, for obedience to God rather than to men curbs power when it goes astray and serves it for the common good.

Spiritual resistance is in no way a renunciation of legitimate defense or of the fight for justice. It is at all times the most legitimate defense, and, in the atomic age, the only one that is reasonable and possible: the only one that does not entail the destruction of what it is pretending to defend.

Spiritual resistance consists in opposing evil, not by an evil of the same nature in the opposite direction, but by an equal and appropriate good.

"For," says the Apostle, "the weapons of our warfare are not carnal, but mighty through God to the pulling down of strongholds."

It is clear that Christians, who have built so many empires and seen so many crumble, cannot at the same time put their trust in spiritual weapons and in the H-bomb.

Informations Catholiques Internationales has published an extract from the draft of an analytical statement on war and peace, at present circulating confidentially. If it were to be adopted, it would do much to fulfill our aspirations.

It contains straightforward declarations such as this: "The massive destruction of whole populations such as the bombing of Hamburg, Leipzig, and Hiroshima is a crime which cries out to heaven for revenge."

Again, "Whoever gives orders contrary to people's rights must expect to be disobeyed."

But if this is so, if total war is a crime, should it not be emphasized that the preparation of that crime is just as much of a crime? Such a statement would be of great and immediate consequence, for whoever works in time of peace on atomic weapons could no longer remain ignorant of his guilt and the need to change his method of earning a living.

Furthermore, every citizen who takes no action in the face of this immediate danger should know that he is guilty and that in speech or in writing or by any other means at his command, he must break the complicity of his silence and wake up before the irreparable happens.

Finally, what in our humble opinion is completely lacking is a statement embodying the four rules of spiritual resistance:

1. That it should be carried out without bloodshed.

2. Without fraud or lies, openly and without evading punishment, but on the contrary, seeking it and bearing it with gentle dignity.

3. With respect for the adversary and his freedom and dignity, and care for his conversion.

4. That it should be testimony to this truth, that sacrifice has a saving virtue (the lesson of the Cross and the tradition of the martyrs).

There should also be a reminder that spiritual resistance has proved its practical efficiency in India, and in different private and public conflicts both in the West and in the East. Its history is not well known and should be studied with attention in these times of extreme peril.

I apologize for the perhaps unnecessary length of these pages. The silent supplication of my total fast might have sufficed to say all this and more, much better than words.

Whatever the case may be, I have gone into seclusion and will remain hidden in the Cistercian convent at Frattocchie. Only a few friends and some dignitaries of the Church know of my fast. I hope the press will not call attention to it.

Trembling, but not without hope, I lay it at Your Holiness's feet and in the heart of our merciful Lord.

Your devoted servant,
LANZA DEL VASTO

The monastery in which Shantidas and Pierre Mohandas found shelter is a big brick building, new, but in sober taste, surrounded by an old olive plantation bordering on the Appian Way at the foot of the Alban Hills. The hostelry is a little red and gray palace where more than one pope has lived. They were given Pope Benedict XIII's vaulted room.

Shantidas received strength from the beautiful services in the high, resounding chapel in the company of the friendly monks and in the care of his son Mohandas who, as everyone knows, is a doctor.

The ordeal passed without accident or anxiety. He came and went, worked and was cheerful to the very last. Meanwhile, Mohandas observed the Trappist rule, was admitted into the choir, and attended the night offices. During the day he visited the lord bishops in their gilded offices and sometimes knocked in vain. Nevertheless, he was fortunate enough to meet guests in the colleges where visiting cardinals are received, and he had some conversations with accredited theologians which were useful in advancing our cause.

But no answer was forthcoming from the Vatican except an

official acknowledgment which came twenty days later. Had the letter reached its destination? It seemed doubtful. Had it been read, understood, and transmitted to the competent council commissions? It was unlikely. Because of the Pope's health, it was impossible to obtain a private hearing so as to find out for certain.

But the fast was working and bearing fruit even at a distance. Letters came from the community and from friends announcing that several were partaking in the sacrifice and through it receiving grace.

On Palm Sunday, Chanterelle, Shantidas's wife, arrived and was of great consolation to her husband. On Holy Wednesday, she visited the secretariat of state, taking with her another letter requesting an answer to the first and a blessing for Holy Week "which is the hardest." The secretary, Monsignor P——, talked with her for over an hour, assuring her that the letter had been read and that there was no answer to be expected. "Actually," he said, "the answer is here!" and he handed her the encyclical *"Pacem in Terris,"* which was to be published the next day. "There are things in it that have never been said, pages that might have been signed by your husband!"

On Good Friday, as Shantidas, somewhat tired, was sunning himself on the terrace, a priest came and visited him. "I've brought you some news from the Vatican," he said, smiling broadly. And he presented him with the Pope's gifts, two leather cases bearing the papal arms and containing a rosary and a medal, with an accompanying message, the special prayer of the Holy Father for Lanza del Vasto and his wife.

On Easter Sunday, friends came by to join the penitent at High Mass and then break the fast with him by taking a little orange juice and cookies. They brought him back to his family and the fresh green of the beautiful garden radiant with Judas trees in bloom, and wisteria climbing to the tops of the cypresses.

There he rested for a week, slowly recovering his strength. At his invitation, friends joined him every evening, and from them he formed the first Roman group of the Ark.

But, to return to the news brought us by the secretary of state, let us see which passages of the encyclical correspond to Shantidas's letter.

Concerning Romans 13 and obedience to established power:

"The powers that are ordained of God," as St. Paul teaches, "for there is no power but of God." The apostle's doctrine is explained by St. John Chrysostom thus: "What do you mean? that everyone in authority is ordained of God? 'That is not what I affirm,' Paul would reply. 'I am not speaking of persons in power, but of their mandate only.'"

Power is above all a moral force. Those who hold it must therefore appeal in the first place to conscience, to the duty incumbent on all to serve the common interest with zeal. But men are all equal in natural dignity; no man has the power to determine in another his inward consent; that power is reserved to God, who alone reads and judges the secret decisions of every man. In consequence, human power can bind consciences only insofar as it is a part of the power of God.

Power, an exigence of moral order, emanates from God. If, therefore, rulers make laws or take measures contrary to moral order, and consequently, to the Divine Will, their so doing cannot oblige consciences, for *we must obey God rather than men.* Furthermore, in such cases, power ceases to be itself and degenerates into oppression. "Human legislation has the character of law only insofar as it conforms to the true reason, which plainly shows that it draws its strength from eternal law. But insofar as it deviates from reason, it is declared unjust. It does not accord with the spirit of the law but is rather a form of violence" (St. Thomas).

"It is not irrelevant," says the encyclical, "to quote St. Augustine's words, 'Once justice has been put aside, what are empires but robbing on a grand scale' (*The City of God*)."

On the subject of the arms race, and in particular, of atomic weapons:

It is customary to justify armament by repeating that under present conditions, peace can only be assured by the balance of armed forces. An increase in the military potential somewhere then makes other states redouble their efforts in the same area, and if one political community is equipped with atomic weapons, this invites others to provide themselves with similar means of equal destructive power.

And so populations live in continual fear as though a terrible storm might strike at any moment. Their fear is not groundless, since the weapons are always ready. It seems incredible that there are men in the world willing to be responsible for the immeasurable massacre and ruin of war. Yet we are forced to admit that a surprise or an accident would be enough to cause the holocaust. Even supposing that the very monstrosity of the effects of modern weapons dissuaded everybody from fighting, unless nuclear tests for military purposes are stopped, it is to be feared that their consequences will be fatal to life on earth.

Justice, wisdom, and a sense of humanity therefore demand an end to the arms race. They demand that in every country the number of weapons be immediately reduced, that atomic weapons are banned, and finally, that disarmament is enforced by common agreement. "We must at all costs prevent world war with its economic and social ruin, its moral and social aberration, from breaking out upon humanity for the third time," says Pope Pius XII.

But let each and all clearly understand that the growth of military power cannot be checked, nor armaments be decreased, much less done away with, unless total disarmament is also carried out in the soul. We must work with one heart and mind to wipe out the fear and psychosis of war. This requires that the fallacy that peace results from the balance of military power should be replaced by the principle that true peace can only be built in mutual trust. We believe that this aim can be achieved since it is at once a necessity for reason, highly desirable, and of the greatest usefulness.

First of all, it is an aim willed by reason. The thing is obvious to all, or at least, should be: "just like relations between individuals, international relations cannot be regulated by the force of arms." They must be ruled by wisdom's measure, that is, the law of truth, justice, and loyalty.

No other choice can be so fruitful. Peace is good for everyone: individuals, families, nations, and the whole of humanity. Pope Pius XII's warning still rings in our ears, "With peace, nothing is lost, but all may be lost by war . . ."

But peace is just an empty word if it is not founded on order, order founded on truth built on justice, given life and fullness by charity and efficient expression by freedom.

What more is there to wish for after these strong, sound words, and what do we hope for from the Council?

The principle of "civil disobedience" having been admitted, it remains to define the method, that is to say, the rules of spiritual resistance or active nonviolence.

6

THE WOMEN'S FAST

WOMAN'S VOICE IN THE COUNCIL

1965

Chanterelle and Shantidas did not arrive until the eve of the opening of the exhibition (September 20). Pierre Mohandas, Jo Pyronnet, and the Stork (Michel Lefeuvre) had gone on ahead of them and everything was in order. We had obtained a vaulted gallery about twenty yards long and five yards wide in a seventeenth-century palace next door to the big church of Saint Agnes, Via dell'Anima (Street of the Soul), overlooking the red Piazza Navona where fountains play among nymphs, bearded rivers, tritons, and writhing marine deities. This palace is the headquarters of Unitas Center where the Council fathers, observers, and experts attend conferences, so that we could not have been better placed.

The exhibition prepared at La Chesnaie by Michel the Stork and his small team was brought to Rome in two suitcases. The greatest feats of nonviolence were commemorated with large photographs. They were placed on big black-and-white or black-and-red squares, pleasing to the eye. The captions were translated into two languages in careful script. There was also a table with books and pamphlets. The text of the exhibition, printed on glossy paper, was handed out to all visitors so that they might reflect on it, and it was sent to the people we were going to visit. For during the ten days that had gone by since the beginning of the fast, we had been going, one by one, or in groups, to talk to the bishops while Jean Goss, whom we met in Rome, was doing the same thing on his own.

We called once more on Cardinal Lercaro, thanks to whom our people had found the convent where they could fast safe from prying eyes. He said some fine things to us that we should have liked to hear ringing out in the Aula. But he was planning to state them when he announced the women's fast, a direct way of reaching the ears of those who are meant to hear without noising the thing abroad.

Together we called on Maximos IV, Patriarch of Antioch, whose contribution to the previous session had been one of the most remarkable. When we entered, he complimented us and remarked on our dress and beards, apparently quite forgetting that his own and those of his surrounding archimandrites were just as picturesque.

"What do you want me to do?" he asked at once. Jo thereupon began to speak to him of nonviolence and did so with eloquence and warmth. But the patriarch, tired of men and convinced by experience that there is nothing to be done, exclaimed, "Yes, I'll put a word in. To be sure. I'll speak out. But oh, my son, oh, my son . . ."

If only we could find a bishop, just one, who would take our cause in hand and make it his own! we sighed.

All received us well, listened kindly and agreed emphatically when it was a question of condemning the great crime and worldwide catastrophe that war is, but "self-defense" was always the stumbling block and no sooner was it mentioned than the chain of reasoning we had at last eagerly broken was soldered anew.

"But Monsignor, is there no other way of defending oneself

against an evil than by committing yet another evil against it? Does one evil right another? What does Jesus Christ say about it? *'Whosoever shall smite thee on the right cheek, turn to him the other also.'* "

"Yes, I know, I know . . . It's a piece of advice."

"And when do we follow it?"

"In private."

"No, Monsignor, neither in private nor in public. Never! Admit it. We do 'nothing more than the heathen' and sometimes *much less!*"

"Alas, it's true, we must admit it."

"And like everybody else, the Church forgets that the only solution is the one given by the Savior. It believes in governments, experts, diplomats, politics, and even the military, but when the Lord speaks, then it is only advice for perfection, strictly private and followed by no one, out of modesty!"

"If we say such things, the nations will not listen to us."

"They never have listened to anything you teach and preach, yet you continue to do it, and know that you must continue. If you have any chance at all of being heard now, it is just on this subject. People expect something better from you than platitudes, ambiguous orders, and idle blessings."

"But, after all, you can't refuse people the right to defend themselves."

At this point, weary of going round and round in circles, we would get up, make a deep bow, and leave.

Jo, however, had struck up a friendship with one of the Council editors. We got hold of a draft of the encyclical. To our satisfaction, the chapter we were concerned with contained the broad outlines of *"Pacem in Terris,"* dealing with the monstrosity of total war, the unacceptable balance of terror, the impossibility of righting wrongs with arms, and we even found a phrase in favor of conscientious objection (the fruit of Jean Goss's labor). But there was no reference to nonviolence. "Our sentence," the one it had been so difficult to get through to the Council during our previous visit and which had been accepted without discussion by the commission, was missing. Perhaps it had been cut out with a whole slice of the text in the course of one of the numerous changes it had already undergone. We were appalled.

Toward the twenty-seventh, the girls arrived, and some old friends who are just as loyal as if they were Companions. One of these was Paul Ruty of Nîmes, who had brought his wife to the fast. After days of fierce storms, it was a Roman autumn; the light was golden and the air sweet and fragrant. Shantidas took a group of girls for a walk in the ruins and the narrow red streets, but Jo the captain called everyone back to reality and gave each group of women a list of the bishops they were to visit before going into seclusion for their fast.

One morning, we were awakened by the telephone. It was Jean Goss, exulting. He had found "our sentence" in the scheme, not in the chapter on war, but in that on peace. Nonviolence was recommended as a solution to social conflict (where it had already proved efficient), but not as a means of parrying and stopping conflict between nations. Our task would therefore be to try to introduce into this chapter a new statement on the subject, however discreet and brief.

Another point worried us: "So long as international institutions remain insufficient" was the gist of the text, "the possession of nuclear weapons for purely defensive purposes cannot be considered illegitimate." This sort of statement rules out all previous proclamations about the criminal character of such weapons and is, moreover, self-contradictory, since these weapons may be used for attack or revenge, but never for defense, neither is there any defense against them.

We wanted the following amendment: "Nations cannot be expected to disarm unilaterally and unconditionally, but they should at least agree to get rid of nuclear weapons which cannot be considered defensive." That would change the declaration of legitimacy into a statement of fact, the fact of a deplorable state of things requiring remedy and not justification.

On the first of October, we accompanied the women to the convent where they were to fast. But let them speak for themselves. Here is their declaration:

IN ROME, IN SUPPORT OF THE COUNCIL
A TEN-DAY TOTAL FAST
BY TWENTY CATHOLIC AND PROTESTANT WOMEN
FROM VARIOUS COUNTRIES

These women know that the Assembly of Council Fathers, confronting a world in danger of annihilation, is going to take the formidable responsibility of stating its views on the problem of war and peace.

As mothers and guardians of life, they have sought a way of participating in the ordeal according to their condition. Urged by the advice of Paul VI to "put themselves into a state of spiritual vigil" and by the encyclical "*Pœnitentiam Agere*" of Pope John XXIII, they will fast and pray for ten days in the seclusion of a convent, entreating the Lord to inspire the Council Fathers with the evangelical solution for which the world is waiting.

But, people will say, is it possible to stop the arms race, give up the balance of terror, and disarm without bringing about a lack of balance, which would favor the unscrupulous and be more dangerous still?

Yes, it is possible, provided destructive weapons are replaced by a different kind of force.

THE WEAPON OF THE POOR

Is it possible to defend justice and enforce recognition of the rights of the weakest without having recourse to means which are the negation of all human and spiritual values?

The fact is that these weapons, belonging to the rich and powerful, can supply no remedy for the most grievous injustices in the present-day world. On the contrary, they only help to make them worse.

In the century of the atomic bomb, it is by the "underdeveloped" and the oppressed that we are reminded of the existence of a weapon within the means of the poorest: nonviolent action or spiritual resistance. The Indians under the guidance of Gandhi and Vinoba, the blacks in the United States in their struggle against segregation, have demonstrated this in a masterly fashion. The influence of these men on the world grows greater day by day. The award of the Nobel Peace Prize to Luthuli, then to King, shows the growing importance of this new force in the building of dynamic peace.

WHAT IS NONVIOLENCE?

The voluntary mobilization of the moral and spiritual force of a nation, nonviolence is a practical rediscovery of the "arms of peace" of which St. Paul speaks, and a concrete application of the force of truth at the community and civic level. Only experience can give an exact idea of it. It is founded on:

An appeal to conscience and respect of the adversary, without fraud or lies;

Resistance to evil and injustice and a refusal to hate, hit, or threaten;

Open disobedience to unjust laws; the acceptance of punishment;

Service for the welfare of all, not excluding the adversary.

It is not a ready-made system where victory is won beforehand, but a combat requiring as much courage, perseverance, and invention as war.

It is bound to be efficient even in an earthly way, since the Gospel assures us that it will, and since the Cross is a sign of victory over evil.

This fast confronts the conscience
of Christians with a double question.

Surely we cannot take responsibility, in the eyes of God and of the generations to come, for conceding any justification whatever to the horror of total war and weapons of wholesale destruction, even used for defensive reprisal.

God grant that we accept the lesson the poorest of our brethren have taught us, whether they be Christian or not! Their victorious nonviolent struggle throws new light on the Sermon on the Mount, revealing it to be not only a way to personal perfection but also a power capable of transforming institutions and giving a new meaning to history.

TAKING PART IN THE FAST

Chanterelle Lanza del Vasto, Companion of the Ark

Marcelle Bernadat, Grenoble

Lise Caillon, Bayonne

Louisette Caramelli, Haute-Savoie

Maryse Chenevey, Companion of the Ark

Dorothy Day, New York

Claude Forcellino, Marseilles
Raymonde Llech, Marseilles
Piéra di Maggio, Companion of the Ark
Edith Maximoff, Companion of the Ark
Erika Mitterer, Vienna
Yvette Naal, Paris
Marianne Platz, Mulhouse
Christiane Pons, Nice
Léa Provo, Antwerp
Rose-Marie Ressouches, Paris
Milène Ruty, Nîmes
Mathilde Seghezzo, Buenos Aires
Nicole Uhl, Paris

*How is it that ye do not discern this time? . . . Except ye
repent, ye shall all likewise perish.*

LUKE 12:56 and 13:3

FROM CHANTERELLE'S DIARY

Friday, October 1
Convent of the Last Supper, Rome

I have given nobody this address, and our own people learned
it only yesterday so as to be at the appointed place this morning.
"Friday at ten o'clock, Via X."

Once through the gate, we found a small group of joyful
women waiting in the courtyard. There were the fasters.

The Mother Superior, tiny under her white hood, her blue
eyes very clear and very deep, came toward me. She is happy
about our fast and says she will pray with us.

We went upstairs to the third floor where we saw twelve

rooms through twelve open doors. Our choice was quickly made. We let Dorothy Day, who is elderly, and Erika Mitterer, the writer, each have a single, sunny room, and the others settled in two by two according to friendships struck up on the spur of the moment or the evening before: for yesterday the fasters visited the bishops in a group and they have already got to know one another.

Unwittingly, Piéra and I also have a room each. Mine is called Santa Felicità. It is true. I have so looked forward to this blessed time of seclusion that I am now in felicity.

Shantidas, all in blue, carries up our suitcases. Jean-Pierre, always obliging, goes off to fetch mineral water. Raoul Ducrocq, our doctor, smiles at us. Yvonne Labande, who will be our link with the outside world, sets off again to listen to the minutes of the morning session dictated day by day to the press by Monsignor Haubtmann.

Cardinal Lercaro has promised to announce our fast to the Council Fathers. Perhaps today? It is so wonderful I scarcely dare believe it.

Our fast is not at all public. It is neither protest nor pressure, but on the contrary, an act of piety, penance, and union. We want it to be made known first, to those to whom it is addressed, the Council Fathers in the Aula. The press will learn about it through them. But the date and time must remain secret in order to avoid vulgar publicity.

We go down into the garden with its broad avenues of pines and, by chance, gather in a grove where the Holy Virgin, hands outstretched, is saying Yes.

She looks as if she were attentive only to the call from on high, but glancing down her gown I see her light foot treading on the serpent. The contrast strikes me.

Yes, that's it. By saying Yes, by being open to what the Lord wills, we crush evil underfoot without even knowing.

Attacking the serpent directly with all our earthly might is often vain, for it rears its head again as soon as we turn our attention away, but if our eyes are fixed on God and we do his will, "all the rest is added unto us" and evil vanishes.

While my thoughts run thus, the prayer is said by Shantidas and the ring of fasting women. Having settled the timetable for the day, we all go off to rest.

And at five o'clock, in the same grove, here we are listening in a group to a reading of the *Commentaire* concerning *Love thine enemies*. The trees are green and shining, the meadow moist and covered with flowers. Round this calm, the city thunders. Effortlessly, we are at one with the peace, forgetting the noise that hems us in. How good it would be always to have in our hearts, in the midst of our restless lives, the same small island and its cool, quiet shade.

At seven o'clock Yvonne comes back. The cardinal has said nothing, not having spoken at the conference. It is well. We can pray on Saturday and Sunday, and hope that on Monday, October 4, the day of St. Francis, the day of Paul VI's journey to New York, the cardinal will announce our fast. God grant that it will move the fathers to consider the "evangelical solution" of the problem, the one everybody seems to ignore, nonviolence.

These last few days, the girls have been doing good work with the bishops. The latter, mostly elderly, were touched by their youthful faces. "You're going to fast, are you?" they said to Claude, Nicole, and Maryse. "Good, very good. We shall pray for you. Come back and see us when it is over."

Mathilde, the Argentine, spent two days visiting all the bishops from her own country.

"What!" said Monsignor Iriarte, "so you're going to speak to me of nonviolence too? In Argentina, at Fortinolmos, I received a parcel of books by Lanza del Vasto with a letter on nonviolence. At Buenos Aires, a letter, a visit, and a book. In

Europe, in Luxemburg, a letter, a book; in Brussels, the same thing. In Rome, it's the Ark once more that calls on me. How many of you *are* there?"

And Mathilde, who came here ill, now feels perfectly well.

FROM LISE CAILLON'S DIARY

Life withdraws from us like a tide, leaving great deserted spaces. Outside, the pine trees shudder and the city moans. You must go down into the garden and lie down at the foot of the trees. Here life surrounds you, the sun bathes the grass and leaves, and through the landscape the light of the Kingdom seems to smile.

A trustful lizard comes and settles on my arm, and immediately flees. Life is a great marvel and this new state which separates us from the world of the living reveals the fragile beauty of the created world.

By and by, in the chapel, we shall descend into inner darkness to rediscover within ourselves the way to the mystery of life, the dwelling where the flame keeps vigil.

May our Lord enlighten these men dedicated to Him, give them courage and a voice. We can only love and give, sustained by invincible hope.

NOTE BY CHANTERELLE

Suffer suffering to come unto me. The big beast spreads itself slowly, astonished.

Usually, people flee it, start up, chase it away. Some remedy makes it recoil or our redoubled activity makes us forget it and then, furious, it lashes out with its sharp claws or its sharper teeth.

Nothing of that here. We let it come in. It lies down full length and stretches out its long legs. Sickness grips you.

Thanks be to God, this is what we wanted. In vain does it weigh on the heart and the pit of the stomach, no one makes a gesture to push it off. Thanks to it, we feel what thousands of human beings feel, weak and starving. Thanks be to God.

Prayer burns the fiercer, the call for help comes from greater depths. One must be weak to become, at last, the child in need of its father.

The big beast yawns with boredom. In the end, it stalks off. Each of the fasters, after a period of melancholy, finds her good humor again and straightens herself again like a flower.

A lesson on nonviolence. Suffer to come unto me, say Yes, understand, suffer, and most conflict disappears. It is the first stage in the great adventure.

Speaking of the adventure, how far have we actually got?

Monday, Tuesday, Wednesday have gone by and nothing has been announced in the Council. But it doesn't matter much to us and we pray tranquilly in our haven of peace, guarded by the two Mothers, the only sharers of our secret.

But suddenly on Thursday, at four o'clock, the Mother Superior arrives in full sail and announces the Bishop of Verdun, Monsignor Boillon. The fasters assemble in my room with the swiftness of birds.

The bishop arrives, homely and good-natured, clad all in black. He sits down and stretches out his legs. "Well," he says, "you know we have passed on to other subjects now; we are dealing with missions. Personally, I feel we haven't talked enough about war. So I have asked to be allowed to speak tomorrow morning on behalf of seventy bishops who have signed my request. I am going to announce your fast, so I've come along to see you and find out all about it."

"Monsignor, it's the Holy Spirit that has sent you," I exclaim.

"Perhaps it is."

And he begins talking to us about his part of the country, Verdun, whose soil is soaked with the blood of millions of men. "They say nobody has a right to kill women and children, but has anyone the right to kill young men and commit such bloody massacres?"

The things he says are just, firm, and wise. We try gently to explain why we are there.

"Oh yes, nonviolence is it? Jo Pyronnet is coming to talk to me about it this evening."

"If you want to find out about it, Monsignor, read this book. Every page is a lesson in living." And I hand him *Why We Can't Wait* by Martin Luther King, Jr.,[1] pencil-marked, underlined, scribbled over with comments during nights of vigil.

Still friendly and simple, he goes off again.

Next day, Friday the eighth, in the Aula of St. Peter's, he read his excellent speech to two thousand Council Fathers and after speaking of evangelical gentleness, read our text.

Thanks to the Bishop of Montpellier, Monsignor Tourel, Shantidas was in St. Peter's that morning and heard the announcement.

When, in September, I had been worrying about the moment when the passage on war and peace would be discussed, he had said to me, "You'll see that everything will be ordained by the hand of God. The discussion will take place during the ten fast days on the day I am in the Vatican."

I had smiled at his naïve conviction, but he had been right.

NOTE BY SHANTIDAS

Yes, there was something miraculous in the perfect success of our plans, which we had dreamed rather than drawn up together.

---

[1] Published by Harper and Row, New York (1964).

But the main instrument of providence had been Father Gauthier, a worker priest from Nazareth, and the author of a fine book, *Console My People*, in which he pleads with all his might for the reduction of the Church to "the Church of the Poor." He had been one of the prime movers of the Pope's journey to the Holy Land and, because of his spiritual prestige, was very influential in Vatican II.

We had become acquainted in a bookshop where he was presenting his book and where Shantidas was giving a talk; strong ties bound them in friendship from the start.

He soon attacked us on our position toward the world of today, but Jo's replies enlightened him on our respective vocations and the link between them, which confirmed our friendship. He visited the fasting women and consoled them with profound insight.

Now he happened to be a close friend of the Bishop of Verdun.

At last we had found the man to espouse our cause!

He was not the only one. Monsignor Alfrinck intervened favorably ("Violence, even when lawful, is not in the spirit of Christ"), so did Christopher Butler, Monsignor Liénard, Monsignor Ancel, Monsignor Duval, and even Cardinal Ottaviani, First Dignitary of the Holy Office, who repeated, to the applause of the assembly, his *"Bellus omnino interdicendum!"* (War is to be utterly forbidden!)

EXTRACT FROM A SPEECH BY THE VERY REVEREND CHRISTOPHER BUTLER, ABBOT OF DOWNSIDE

1. According to our text, "so long as international organizations are unable to safeguard peace, it cannot be said that it is in itself

unlawful to possess modern weapons for the sole purpose of keeping a similarly armed adversary under restraint."

I suggest that this passage be deleted from the document. Nobody thinks that the great powers merely *possess* such arms. The fact is that on each side of the curtain, there is a system of preparation for the use of such arms, their unlawful use, should total war come about. If we think such preparation legitimate, better to say so openly and not hide behind a reference to the simple "possession" of these weapons.

But should we not go on saying clearly that not only is it unlawful to make use of such preparation by waging war, but that the mere intention to make use of it even if a "conditional" intention, is seriously immoral? It is inopportune to implicate in this manner the intentions of heads of state or those of their subordinates and the population in general.

It is ridiculous to ask if such preparations are conceivable without there being at least a conditional intention to use nuclear weapons. It is fairly obvious that the intention to wage war unjustly is in itself unjust enough.

2. Obedience to the government and commanding officers in time of war. It would be preferable not to speak in this context of "presumed to be right"[2] in favor of those who give orders. Although true in theory, this presumption has caused numerous crimes, as recently, when subordinates obeyed diabolical orders. Moreover, today, all men have a moral duty not only toward their own country, but toward the whole human race. They are called on, properly speaking, to obey a world authority which doesn't yet exist, but which is necessary for their common welfare. So, instead of insisting on a "presumption of rightness," which can so easily lead to sin, it would be better to declare emphatically that duty may sometimes oblige us to refuse to obey.

[2] This thesis, which is classic, makes it a duty for a subordinate to suppose in cases of doubt that his superiors are right.

3. I am glad the text mentions conscientious objection, but dislike the phrase which implies that objectors are somehow immature. It would be better to speak only of objection founded on authentic reasons of conscience. Certain conscientious objectors are perhaps in truth the prophets of truly Christian morality.

In conclusion, let us take advantage of this opportunity to state clearly that the Church, God's people, does not seek to be protected from its enemies, whoever they may be, by war, much less by modern warfare. We are the mystic body and Christ is our head. He refused to defend himself or defend his mission with his disciple's sword, or even with hosts of angels, ministers of justice, and the love of God. The arms of the Gospel are not nuclear, but spiritual. They win victory, not by war, but by suffering. Let us therefore have sympathy for the leaders of state in their struggle with immense difficulties. Let us acknowledge their good intentions with gratitude. But let us add these few words to remind them that desirable ends do not justify immoral means, neither do they justify the conditional intention to stand up to an immoral attack with immoral defense. Our power lies in the Name of the Lord who created heaven and earth.

Note—The Very Reverend Father Abbot visited the women who were fasting and, deeply moved, he thanked them. "We were all in need of this penance," he said. "The Council is not a meeting of dignitaries laying down the law, it is you! It is God's people suffering, hoping, and praying."

EXTRACT FROM A SPEECH
BY PIERRE BOILLON,
BISHOP OF VERDUN

We, O venerable fathers, have only one message to give, in the name of the Lord, in the face of the nations, and that is to cry out, like our most holy Pope Paul, "Ye are brethren in Christ, ye shall not wage war!"

We in this Council must add that the monstrous wars waged on one another by the Western nations, whom the world calls Christian, are a major obstacle to the acceptance of the Gospel by the nations who ignore Christ. Let us make sure that by making distinction between "lawful and unlawful" we do not allow this scandal to take place again and again.

Furthermore, as has already been said several times, it is necessary not only to condemn war but also to build peace, for which an international authority is needed. But institutions are not enough. Public opinion, that is to say, the conscience of the nations, must be educated for that purpose. And it is mainly the business of the Church that such education should be moral, or rather, evangelical. Let me be more precise:

Humility on an international scale. Let citizens and heads of nations acknowledge limits to national sovereignty and independence, where international authority takes over. Woe betide pride, even national pride!

Poverty on an international scale. Let the wealthiest nations and their wealthiest citizens share their wealth and their way of living with the poorest nations instead of increasing the fortune of the wealthy in vile fashion by war!

Meekness which is the admirable sign of Christ himself. Meekness on an international scale is the absolute refusal by mankind of the violence of arms: they bear testimony to meekness who practice and bring about nonviolent action with courage and with suffering, but acting without violence whether within a nation or between nations.

Among these (since in this Aula we are talking of war) there are twenty lay women, in Rome itself, abstaining from all food for ten days and praying that the Holy Spirit will illuminate us. Allow me to let them have their brief say.

At this point, he read in French the women's declaration (see pages 178–181).

For the first time, the voice of women had made itself heard under the vault of St. Peter's.

EPILOGUE TO THE FAST IN ROME

The women's fast in Rome was followed by the Friends of the Ark, not only in thought but in deed. First to deserve mention was the group in Buenos Aires, where fourteen persons fasted for the ten days. Akos, our Hungarian friend, did the same, all alone in his house at Mougins, and so did Pierre Almand of Annecy and several others who wish not to be named. As for Léa Provo, head of the Antwerp group, she left Rome without breaking her fast and went on fasting ten days longer in her own country. Almost all the groups in France, Switzerland, Belgium, and Spain fasted in relays and sent letters to their bishops: some of them were very fine and received a reply.

Dorothy Day, who to our great joy came and fasted in Rome with our girls, returned to New York as soon as the ten days were over and related the adventure in the columns of *The Catholic Worker.*

Our friends in Paris fasted for three days. The parish of St. Séverin, whose community of priests has been on friendly terms with the Ark for twenty years, welcomed the fasters and supported them. The fast was announced and commented on from the pulpit at every Mass that Sunday.

STATEMENTS BY THE COUNCIL

We now have before us the first translations of Schema XIII which, after three revisions and corrections, and final approval by vote, bears the name of Pastoral Constitution on the Church in the World of this Time.

We immediately plunged into Chapter V: "The Safeguard of Peace," for which we had undertaken three journeys to Rome, two long fasts, and exerted ourselves in numberless ways, without counting the fasts, letters, and visits of our friends to their bishops.

We saw at once:

1. That "our" sentence concerning nonviolence was in it, somewhat abridged but in a very good place, right in the introduction.

2. That blind obedience leading to acts contrary to "people's rights" is condemned and that the fathers "warmly praise the courage of those who openly resist the authorities who order such actions."

3. That governments are invited to make "humane legal arrangements" for conscientious objectors.

4. That total war is condemned "firmly and without hesitation."

5. That any act of war aiming at the indiscriminate destruction of whole towns and vast regions with their inhabitants "is a crime against God and men."

6. That the "balance of terror" is a fallacy, and far from removing the causes of war, is liable to aggravate them more and more.

7. That the "arms race" is a wound inflicted on humanity. "It does the poor intolerable harm, and there is every reason

to fear that its continuation will bring about the disasters for which it is already preparing the means."

Although nuclear weapons are not condemned in an explicit and particular manner (they are condemned along with every means of wholesale destruction), their "possession" is at least not called lawful, as we found to our horror in the earlier version.

We can therefore tell our friends the good news that the aims of our three missions to Rome have been achieved, thanks to us or to others—it doesn't matter; thanks to God.

The protests, motions, and intrigues of quite a number of American and other bishops in an attempt to cut out one or other of the seven points or to get their venerable colleagues to refuse the whole of Schema XIII and the remarks of a certain Italian bishop on the "immorality" of conscientious objection were only the last contortions of the Devil being vanquished by the Spirit.

We shall return to this important text which is so dear to our heart and quote and comment on it later. Our friends are invited to read it and rejoice. And to use it without delay in order to defend peace in word and thought.

Before reading it ourselves, we met so many people disappointed by it that we might have thought it feeble, timorous, and ambiguous, as ecclesiastical language so often is on these subjects. But in fact, Chapter V of the "Pastoral Constitution" is in almost none of its articles behind John XXIII's encyclical *"Pacem in Terris"* and in some respects, is ahead of it. I should define the "Constitution," taken all in all, as an act of courage and good will.

The Council, at its close, appealed to all the women in the world, entrusting to them the primordial task of "reconciling men to life."

"Above all, we entreat you, watch over the future of our race. Restrain the hand of man which, in a moment of madness, might attempt to destroy human civilization."

7

A BRIEF
ACCOUNT
OF NONVIOLENCE
IN THE WEST

Nonviolence has a long history in the West. It has had its apostles, its heroes, its theoreticians, its poets and revolutionaries. It has won victories, no doubt less famous than Gandhi's in India, but great and decisive nevertheless; they provide food for thought and hope.

THE CHARTER OF NONVIOLENCE

The Gospel is the Western charter of nonviolence.

"Blessed are the weak, for they shall inherit the earth."

"Love thine enemies, bless them that hate thee."

"And unto him that smiteth thee on the one cheek offer also the other: and him that taketh away thy cloak forbid not to take thy coat also."

"Put up again thy sword into his place: for all they that take the sword shall perish with the sword."

These are the clauses of the Charter, in the original text, such as they were given, without explanation: they are enough for whoever has ears to hear and need no other commentary than the deeds and gestures of the giver, above all, the supreme act of His Passion.

The Christian who refuses, neglects, or forgets the nonviolent teaching contained in these clauses takes away the flame from the fire Jesus came to bring on earth, blunts the point of His sword, and makes the salt lose its savor.

NONVIOLENCE, THE METHOD OF THE MARTYRS

The acts of the first Christians have been a subject of veneration for us since childhood, rather than matter for critical reflection.

Yet if we look upon their steadfast attitude as a method, we see it as what Thoreau and Gandhi called civil disobedience. Their culminating and decisive gesture was the refusal to sacrifice to idols,[1] generally corroborated by other refusals, refusal to go to law in self-defense, refusal to defend themselves in court, refusal to have private property, to accede to power, to carry weapons.

This resistance earned them the criticism of the civilized world, including such great thinkers as Tacitus, Marcus Aurelius, and Plotinus. In the eyes of worldly wisdom, it must be said that the refusal to burn incense to idols appears quite senseless. If the idol is a lump of wood or metal, and incense just a little smoke, easy obligation is a vain and empty gesture, but one which has its use in calming a stupid, hostile crowd. How

---

[1] The refusal was sometimes accompanied by the breaking of statues. Note here, as in India, the aggressive, provoking, vehement side of nonviolence which, need it be said, has nothing to do with nonresistance, the force of inertia or resignation to fate, submission to injustice, lying or the excesses of other people, but is by definition a resistance to evil by the force of the Spirit (Satyagraha).

much more vain and even crazy to refuse the gesture and thus expose the community to losing its best leaders one after the other. Already too few, these guardians of an infinitely precious heritage would be decimated.

But here as elsewhere, worldly prudence shows itself to be negative, presumptuous, blind, incapable of grasping reality in its depth, and so, incapable of foreseeing even the immediate future. Nonviolence alone has proved itself clearsighted and efficient. Adopted by a united group, aware of the principles of its doctrine, its mystic value, the personal discipline and the practical and social consequences involved, nonviolence conquered and overthrew the ancient world and turned it upside down, each barbaric tribe in its turn. As the barbarians advanced, nonviolence overcame them.

ATTILA BEFORE THE LIONS AND WOLVES OF NONVIOLENCE

Wave upon wave of barbaric invasions had broken the dikes of the Roman Empire when the great tidal wave arose that swept everything before it—Attila with his innumerable and irresistible horsemen. It was said that where he had passed, the grass grew no more.

Now, "the Scourge of God" collided with nonviolence twice, and, the second time, was smashed.

The first time was at Troyes, whose walls he had taken by assault. He entered the cathedral where the population had taken refuge to be near their bishop, St. Loup. As he came in, he could see only their backs, for all had fixed their gaze on the holy wafer which the priest was raising. In presence of the mighty silence, the conqueror stood dumbfounded. He withdrew, called his men, and left the city without looting it.

The following year, he invaded Italy and swooped down on Rome where, as a youth, he had been held hostage. He meant to inflict revenge upon it equal to the wound inflicted on his pride. A river barred the way but he soon found a ford and was pushing his horse across it when, on the opposite bank, he caught sight of a body of men marching toward him, armed, not with spears, but with a single crucifix. They were headed by Pope Leo I, wearing the tiara and riding a mule. They were singing as they advanced. The barbarian lost countenance, turned about, and never returned.

NONVIOLENCE, FOUNDATION OF THE CHURCH

When the Church became a sovereign body and every man could enter it without difficulty or risk, the spirit of the world entered it too and the "Prince of this world" had his revenge. The Christian Church treated with the powers of this more or less Christianized world and herself became a worldly power more or less like the others. Nonviolence and evangelical poverty (there can never be the one without the other), the spirit of prophecy, the gift of healing, miracles, and divine grace became proportionately rarer. There were Papal armies, Papal prisons, crusades, burnings at the stake, religious wars, the justification of national or colonial wars, oppression and repression of all kinds. These facts cannot be denied and it is not our intention to defend them or to attack them either. Notwithstanding, we maintain that they are an accidental and temporal aspect of things. The authentic, permanent doctrine of the Church remains peace-loving to its roots and rises above divisions of race, nation, or class. It is respectful of nature and humanity, and moderate. So is its essential structure. No dignity can be won in it by arms; its authority is exercised without coercion.

Its highest title is the childish and familiar one of "Papa," wherein it differs from all empires and all republics. The immense riches it handles come solely from contributions similar to the taxes every state levies on its subjects, but here again the difference is striking, for in all regimes, taxes can only be extracted because of fear of the penalties the slightest delay incurs, whereas the Church, in all her splendor, remains a beggar at the corner of the street.

AMONG THE SAINTS AND IN SECTS

The scarcity of evangelical virtues in the main body of Chistendom has from time to time made men awaken and return. In every century, two kinds of men have arisen whose history is that of nonviolence in the West: the saints who bring about reform, and the founders of sects.

They are opposite and similar to each other. The former correct the Church from within, renew it with their flame, found an order, a work, a spiritual school; the latter rebel or get expelled and seek to found a new church, like that of the early days. But more often than not, the saint, obedient to God rather than to men, is taken for a heretic or a rebel, undergoes persecution and condemnation, and is canonized only after being put to death, whereas the heresiarch sometimes manifests the virtues, the fervor, the purity and charity, and the charisma which characterize the saint.

The most famous sect of the Middle Ages was that of the Albigensians who called themselves Catharists, or the Pure, and did indeed practice purity and nonviolence. They were utterly destroyed by a war which cut off the lovable civilization of Provence in its flower. One might look upon this tragedy as a total failure for nonviolence. But there are two things which prove that this is not so. The first is that it was not a matter of nonviolent resistance wiped out by brutal force, but of a war in which violence was unleashed on both sides. The second is that under the same heading of Albigensians, we put two kinds of men who, to their misfortune, were only too separate, on the one hand, the tiny number of "pure" or "perfect," and on the other, the great flock of people they had cut off from the Church without admitting them to their communion, considering them unworthy, and whom their over-pure doctrine, with its rejection of everything pertaining to nature and the flesh, deprived of all help, happiness, and hope.

It was not the nonviolence of the Catharists, but the violence and impurity of their defenders which lost both sides.

Then came the Renaissance of the pagan gods, and the Reform and the wars of religion. People fought with each other to see who was the better Christian, and it seemed obvious that the better was the one who killed the other. But sects arose to reform the Reform, and saints to prevent the Gates of Hell from prevailing.

There were Mennonites and Mormons, the Amish of Holland, the Dukhobors of Russia, the Hutterites of Switzerland and Germany, all of whom sought refuge from persecution on American soil, where they formed peaceful and fraternal closed communities. Today, in France we have Jehovah's Witnesses, Adventists, and Friends of Man.

A special place must be given to the Quakers and their preaching and tribulation in Christian lands, so like that of the early Christians in the Jewish synagogues of the pagan world. One of them, William Penn, in the course of his adventure in the country of forests which still bears his name, showed how savages can be approached with intent other than their massacre, subjugation, or perversion under the cover of conversion and civilization; that they can be approached in a friendly and trusting manner.

The Jesuits of Paraguay demonstrated this even more fully and in a more lasting and admirable way in their "reductions," where they protected the natives from slavery and corruption, sharing the work and the responsibilities, distributed goods without payment, made possible the free election of native leaders, and set up an organization of independent rural workers and craftsmen which Gandhi and Vinoba had hoped to establish in India under the name of "Gramraj."

THE REVOLUTIONARY NONVIOLENCE OF THE NINETEENTH CENTURY

The nineteenth century saw the beginning of the holy wars of social revolution. It is no longer the charity of Christ or the glory of God, but the happiness of humanity which became the legitimate pretext for collective and systematic manslaughter. A few solitary men were of the opinion that to achieve such a desirable purpose, there must be better means than intrigue, plots, the overthrow of rulers, murder and terror, that in order to achieve justice and peace, just and peaceful means should be found, that these means remained the best, even if they were slow and more difficult: but that being more logical, they might also be simpler and more expedient. The doctrine of civic nonviolence was born. It had its great apostles at the two extremities of the West: in America, Thoreau; in Russia, Tolstoy. The name of John Ruskin of England may be added. (Gandhi drew from these three sources. Apart from the Gospel and the Gita, he found in them almost all the elements of his thought.)

Thoreau had meditated on the immortal pages of Etienne de La Boétie, *Of Voluntary Bondage (Discours sur la servitude volontaire*), written in the middle of the sixteenth century, and he discovered the point at which the pressure of direct nonviolent action must be brought to bear. La Boétie is astonished at the eagerness and zeal with which, unlike unreasoning animals, man subjugates himself. Indeed, those who wield the power that oppresses him have only the power he grants them. Tyrants, of themselves, can do nothing: their subjects make them powerful by believing them to be so. As for the soldiers tramping heavily through fields and towns, they are the people who grind down the people on behalf of the established powers.

From which Thoreau draws the conclusion that the citizen who obeys laws and orders without asking questions does only half his duty and often does the contrary of his duty. For whenever the law functions against justice, whenever it pleases a leader to turn into a despot, the citizen serves as an instrument and accomplice. For his own good, and for the good of all, he too must therefore learn "civil disobedience."

When men unite in sufficient number and apply this principle boldly and strictly, they develop considerable power. Any enslaved nation can be freed from its occupiers without striking a blow, armies can be undone without a battle, an oppressed class can be righted without setting up barricades, a regime overthrown without hanging anyone from the lamp posts, financial corruption can be prevented and wars stopped, as Gandhi and others were to prove.

THE EMPEROR OF HUNGARY IN CHECK,
A FUNERAL REBELLION IN POLAND,
AND THE CHRIST OF THE ANDES

In the second half of last century, the Hungarians, who were under the yoke of Austria, methodically turned away from the

Viennese government and saw to their own public education, legal procedures, and industrial and agriculture production, and refused to buy Austrian goods or pay taxes. The seizures and forced sales which ensued cost more than they brought in. The police, the law courts, the prisons were overwhelmed by the numbers of honorable delinquents. The forces of order came and were billeted throughout the country. The officers were lodged and fed, but not a soul spoke to them. Thereupon, the Emperor of Austria saw fit to impose compulsory military service on the Hungarians and once more met with total refusal. In 1857, after five years of struggle, but without a drop of bloodshed, the Hungarians got their own way.

At the same time, Poland was groaning under the boot of Russia. In vain did she entreat the Czar to give her a parliament. The uprising which then took place might well be called the Funeral Rebellion. When the funeral procession of a patriot poet appeared to be endless, the police became uneasy. They ordered the mourners to disperse, but the procession went on. Then the police launched a cavalry attack, but the procession, leaving its dead and wounded on the pavement, formed anew and continued until nightfall. All the dead who had fallen that day were given similar funerals. The whole nation went into mourning for a year. As a result, Poland obtained a parliament from the Czar. Counter-proof: three years later, Poland had recourse to armed revolt, and the Russians, who asked for nothing better, crushed it.

When relations between Argentina and Chile deteriorated, the two armies marched toward each other through the high passes in the Andes. But on each side, a bishop went ahead of the troops. The bishops met and exchanged the kiss of peace in the sight of the soldiers. And instead of fighting, they sealed a pact of alliance and perpetual friendship between the two nations. A statue of Christ, His hand raised in blessing, stands on the mountain to commemorate this victimless victory.

MORE RECENT FEATS

Here are some of the feats of nonviolence in the West during this century.

In 1909, the women of Spain hindered the unpopular Moroccan war by lying across the rails in front of the trains that were to transport troops. In 1914, a million workmen prevented the government in Madrid from entering the war on the Allies' side.

In 1950, Vienna, devastated and ruined by the war, was divided into four zones, of which the largest was allotted to the Russians. The Soviets thought the small, enslaved, and demoralized country was going to fall into their hands like a ripe fruit. They had the order given for a general strike which was to furnish the pretext for their occupying the country completely. The crowd of workers on their way to work found Floritzdorfer Bridge cut off by barricades, behind which armored tanks were massed. For some time, the human wall and the steel wall stood face to face. Then, in silence, the human wall went forward, the barricades were swept away, and the armored tanks retreated.

In Africa, Nkrumah, inspired by Gandhi, freed his country, Ghana, from the English.

THE MISSION
AND PASSION OF KIMBANGU

After ecstasy, a fall, an illness, and a dream, Simon Kimbangu, a young black Christian of the Congolese Baptist Church, moved by the Spirit, went as if in spite of himself to a neighboring village where a child lay dying, pushed aside the weeping women, began to pray, and laid his hands on the child, who was immediately healed.

Other sick people were brought to him and were healed at his touch.

This was in 1921 when Kimbangu was about thirty years old, and from then on, his village became a seat of pilgrimages, spiritual retreat, and miracles. Whole trainloads of black people came, laboring under the weight of their invalids and sometimes of their dead.

Day and night, crowds surrounded the holy man, praying, singing, imploring, beside themselves with joy and exultation, or eagerly listening to his teaching as they squatted in a ring around him.

For he taught and preached. He knew the Bible thoroughly and never departed from it. He proscribed fetishes, lascivious dancing, and polygamy.

His followers threw their amulets into the fire, split their drums, even burned the rosaries and medallions given out by missions and sometimes smashed the plaster statues of the good fathers. It was like a tumultuous wave sweeping over the country, or rather, an undertow and a flight.

The planters' laborers melted away; at the oil refinery, it was worse than a strike. The shopkeepers waited in vain for customers, the poor vicar searched for his flock, the boy threw down his duster and left, the cook let the pan and the sauce burn on the stove.

The whole colony was indignant, complaints reached Brussels itself, but in vain, for capitals are all the same, each just as ready, on the slightest political or legal or sentimental pretext, to expose their pioneers overseas to ruin, to the fanatical hatred of the savages, even to extermination. And now Brussels, willfully blind, could not see anything wrong. Pretending that the Congo was as free as Belgium to follow its own religion, it took no interest in the superstition which was disturbing the peace and undermining trade, hindering work, emptying hospitals, upsetting quiet citizens, and which, in consequence, resembled subversion.

In short, one can only depend on one's own strength. So (for colonies are the same everywhere) a military court was set up, and within a fortnight, it put a stop to all the miracles, ecstasy, conversions, and prophecy, and dealt with the exceptional case by meting out the well-deserved death sentence.

The complete satisfaction of decent people was foiled only by the intervention of the capital: the wretch was reprieved by King Albert.

And the righteous man, chained by the neck, whipped and clubbed, was taken off to hard labor where he died thirty years later. Thirty-seven thousand of his followers accompanied him, many of them had not awaited arrest to do so, but had presented themselves and their families to the police, insisting on martyrdom.

The church Simon Kimbangu founded in spite of himself proclaims itself nonviolent.

It is composed of Catholics and Protestants who have never revolted against their church but have been driven from their parishes and whose children have been excluded from schools and church clubs.

It underwent such severe persecution that its members eventually hid in the forest.

One day, six hundred of them met in a clearing and unanimously resolved to send a letter to the government announcing that they were going to come into town, being weary of living like hunted beasts; that, like all Christians, they looked upon death as deliverance, and therefore begged for the mercy of all being shot together. The letter ended with blessings.

They assembled in the Baudouin Stadium at the appointed hour. The army barred the way. But the military, instead of taking aim, as the Kimbanguists were expecting, gave their leaders an invitation from the governor. As a result of their interview with him, all the prohibitions were ended, and they were able to celebrate their cult and live and work freely. In the throes of revolution as in tribal rivalry, they have behaved like Christians. They live as brotherly communities disciplined by wise rules. Difficult questions are dealt with by the old men who reach their decisions and their answers by praying together, night and day. There are about five million of them.

IN THE CONGO AND IN COLOMBIA

It should not be forgotten that the movement for the liberation of the Congo, the Abako, had put the country on the path to freedom by the properly Gandhian means of boycott and parallel government. Its declarations were simple, proud, and just.

The massacres and destruction which followed the coming of independence wiped out all memory of the movement and the good it had done.

There was at one time, in Chile, a dictator who was also a general and ruled over the army, the police, and all public authorities.

Now, as sometimes happens, a child had been killed by the police.

Thereupon a funereal revolution broke out. The whole city of Santiago walked in file after the little coffin.

The dictator, watching the convoy from behind the curtained window of his palace, saw that the wisest thing to do was to flee.

He was an intelligent dictator. So intelligent that ten years later he came back to power and, having benefited by the lesson, this time governed in a very respectable manner.

In Colombia, in May 1957, the "best armed dictatorship in the hemisphere" collapsed in one day in face of the unanimous resistance of the population—in particular, that of the women, who gave themselves up to arrest en masse. On the following day, the dictator abdicated. Yet another intelligent dictator. Who would have believed there were so many!

LUTHULI

With exemplary courage, moderation, and dignity, with stubborn goodwill and Christian fervor, Luthuli, the Zulu chief from Groutville, has waged his nonviolent battle in South Africa. It was there that Gandhi led his first and most brilliant campaign. Since the departure of the British, the vice of Apartheid has tightened its grip on the natives, locking them into narrow, barren reserves where hunger, disease, and despair rule.

Luthuli's "Defiance Campaign," his boycotts, trials, and imprisonment have called down the censure of the whole world on the heads of his persecutors.

In his book *Let My People Go*, he tells how, at Camberdown, "Holding white flags and carrying neither sticks nor stones, the women approached the native Commissioner with their demands. The police met them. Almost at the same moment the order to disperse and the order for a baton charge were given. The women were beaten. At Ixopo, where there was some very efficient organization, the women met this threat with a tactic of their own. When the order to disperse was given, they fell down on their knees and began to pray! The police hung around helplessly."

In the epilogue to the book, he writes, "But the struggle goes on, bans, banishments, deportations, gaol or not. We do not struggle with guns and violence, and the Supremacist's array of weapons is powerless against the spirit. The struggle goes on as much in gaol as out of it, and every time cruel men injure or kill defenceless ones, they lose ground. The Supremacy illusion is that this is a battle of numbers, a battle of race, a battle of modern armaments against primitive. It is not. It is right against wrong, good against evil, the espousal of what is twisted, distorted, and maimed against the yearning for health. They rejoice in what hurts the weak man's mind and soul. They embrace what hurts their own soul."

PIERRE CÉRÉSOLE, DOROTHY DAY, AND DANILO DOLCI

The lonely, obscure, and silent sacrifice of conscientious objectors in every country in Europe and America cannot solve the problem of war, of which the army is only an instrument, not the cause. Refusal to fight does not touch the perennial root of war. But at least objectors have gained recognition for one of man's fundamental rights, a right which democracy crushes underfoot as not even the barbaric empires did: the right not to kill.

The Swiss Pierre Cérésole was one of the first objectors. He refused not only armed service, but also war taxes, and gave up an inheritance to wander all over the world, helping whoever gave him shelter. At the end of the First World War, he turned conscientious objection from a negative into a positive thing by setting up the International Voluntary Civil Service in opposition to compulsory military service. This organization comes to the aid of populations in distress from whatever cause, but especially war. This peace army is small indeed for the mighty struggle which, till it came into existence, had not even begun, for lack of fighters.

Smaller still, the Working Order of the Ark is unique in one thing: it is at the same time a working order and a school of inner life, where nonviolence is practiced in all spheres—religion, education, medicine, social relations, the law, economy, food, dress, and aesthetics.

In the United States, a group of Catholics led by Dorothy Day and Ammon Hennacy publish a newspaper called *The Catholic Worker.* They attract attention by their daring, their charity and common sense (which acquires for them a reputation for craziness). Every year, they commemorate and do penance for the crime of Hiroshima by a public fast. They refuse to do military service and to pay war taxes, they invade bomb-testing areas, suffer imprisonment by the police and the burning down of their homes by neighbors. They live in voluntary poverty, found shelters for tramps, create communities in the country, and are guilty of other similar eccentricities.

Then from Sicily came the bandit of all bandits, the most awkward enemy of the blissful tranquility of decent people, the bandit Danilo Dolci. Thoroughly kind, perfectly simple, young yet wise, patient, and built like an ox, it is not too much to say that he is of the stuff that Gandhi was made of. In his dedication to the rescue of the poor he is ever-present and ever-ready to help. In this, and in his fasting and appeal for aid throughout the world, his work is akin to that of Abbé Pierre and Dr. Schweitzer, who also have their part in the history of revolutionary nonviolence because of the questions they raise in every conscience and that spark of loving anger in them which can never be lacking from the force of truth.

IN NORWAY

The invasion of peaceful Norway in April 1940, was rapid and the occupation fairly lenient, to start with.

Underground resistance sprang up immediately. Treachery too, in the shape of the Quisling government and the Hird, the Norwegian Gestapo.

Quisling planned to copy fascist corporations. Teachers' trade unions were dissolved, and the teachers enrolled in the new corporation. At the same time, scholars aged from ten to eighteen were enrolled in a *"sameling,"* an imitation of the Hitler Youth Association.

Out of twelve thousand teachers, between eight and ten thousand mailed letters of resignation on the same day, February 20, 1942.

On the twenty-fourth, the bishops of the state church also resigned, without abandoning their religious duty.

On the twenty-fifth, the government threatened all those who had resigned with fines and lawsuits, and announced the closing of all schools "for lack of fuel."

Fuel flowed into the schools, as did financial aid to the unemployed patriots, while the postmen delivered tens of thousands of complaints and demands due to the closing of the schools.

On March 20, a thousand teachers were arrested, 650 of whom were put into the camp at Grini; then they were transported from camp to camp in cattle trucks, always farther toward the north and the snow.

They were forced to shovel the snow, to undergo the "drill" of dragging themselves through it on their bellies, and to endure the psychological hardships of orders and counterorders howled through loudspeakers—scientific brutality intended to break the will and destroy reason. Every week, they were summoned to withdraw their protests and go back to their posts "willingly."

Some fell ill and were removed, but very few yielded.

Weighed down by chores and great and petty wretchedness, the difficulties of obtaining a bit of bread to eat and a little warmth, they were far from imagining that at that very moment Norway was exalting them as heroes, and that, as time went by, people were thinking of them more and more.

Meanwhile, the schools had opened again and the other teachers had gone back to work, but refused the corporation system. They reacted to official orders with obstinate stupidity, asked for explanations and explanations of explanations.

Quisling, exasperated, roared with rage and vexation. Finally, Hitler intervened to put a stop to the "experiment."

Just when the deadly polar night was about to fall on them, the captives were brought home by sea. Wherever they put into port, flowers and food were lavished on them, in spite of shortages.

The people who headed this exemplary resistance had only vague notions of nonviolence drawn from their earlier reading. They discovered all the rules under the double pressure of events and the strength of their conviction. The unanimity of the combatants and their readiness to grasp veiled orders and carry them out exactly were the main factors in their success.

IN DENMARK

Sometimes people ask, "What could the nonviolence of the Jews do against their persecution by the Nazis?"

The answer is: nothing.

Which does not mean that nonviolence could do nothing for them. But it was up to others to defend the Jews with it.

"Whosoever shall smite thee on the right cheek, turn to him

the other also," means, "Whosoever shall smite thy brother on the cheek, turn to him thine own straightaway."

It was the duty of Christians to present their cheeks. They did so rarely, except in Denmark and in Holland.

Denmark was occupied without a blow being struck. The old king had kept his throne and, to stave off the worst, kept on good terms with the occupying forces.

As soon as he learned that Jews were compelled to wear the yellow star, he went for his usual walk through the streets of the capital, his buttonhole decorated with "the sacred sign, dear to all those who believe in the Scriptures," and thus set the fashion. The Nazis did not relish the gesture, but did not know what to do about it and so delayed persecution.

But as it loomed near, seemingly inevitable, the king sent a message to his cousin in Sweden, appealing to his legendary hospitality in favor of "our citizens in difficulty," and had all Jewish families put on board ship at night.

In Holland at the same time, the manager of a theater, pushed onto the stage by stormtroopers, had to declare that the curtain would not rise till all Jews had left the theater.

The whole audience left, and the curtain did not rise.

That is the kind of thing the great multitude of decent people could have done instead of venting their indignation to no purpose, and this great tide of horror would have been stemmed.

THE SACRIFICE OF PASTOR KING

(After these lines were written, in 1958, Martin Luther King's movement took on proportions comparable to those of Gandhi's Satyagraha.)

There were innumerable gatherings, marches across the country, the picketing of shops forbidden to blacks, and entry into restaurants which refused to serve them. The dignity of these sons of slaves, dignity as great as their courage when clubbed and hosed with water and corrosive acid, was admired by the whole world. In defense of the honor of our race, it should be said that a number of white people entered their ranks and underwent the same ill-treatment.

The leader suffered legal prosecution, imprisonment, insult, threats, and bomb attacks, and died in the prime of life. The movement, decapitated, was submerged by the brutal anger of Black Power and, above all, by the inertia of the masses. A victory for violence, people will say. But let us wait for the end and see who wins in such victories.

PRAGUE

Nonviolent Czech resistance of Russian occupation was unanimous and spontaneous. It apparently had no leader. It disconcerted the invader for many months, then ended by giving in to systematic pressure—yet another victory that scarcely profits the victors. For it lost them supporters in all countries, caused internal dissension, and unmasked their imperialism and their tyranny in the eyes of those to whom the crushing of Hungary had not been sufficient.

THE EASTER MARCHES

In England, an unarmed attack on atomic energy centers took place a few months after our invasion of Marcoule.

Every year after that, a march inspired by Canon Collins (canon of St. Paul's Cathedral) took place at Easter on the atomic energy plant at Aldermaston. A huge crowd filled Trafalgar Square to hear him speak. But unfortunately their rowdiness and their lack of self-control and of seriousness discredited a great cause.

The elderly Lord Bertrand Russell, laying aside his scientific pursuits and his dignity, sat on the sidewalk and got himself jailed in an attempt to dissuade mankind from suicide, but all in vain.

AGAINST THE WAR IN VIETNAM

In the United States, Vietnam war-resisters refused military service in tens of thousands. (I am not referring to desertion, which the morals of nonviolence condemns.) They went in for bigger and bigger mass demonstrations and burned piles of draft cards on Fifth Avenue. Some invaded recruiting offices and soiled the index cards with blood. Some forced their courage to the point of fasting for a hundred days; others poured gasoline over themselves and burned alive, like the bonzes of Saigon. The decisive action that ends such wars does not take place on the battlefield but on the sidewalks of the capital.

THE OBJECTORS
WIN THEIR STATUTE

In France, concurrently with the campaign of voluntary imprisonment in favor of conscientious objectors, Louis Lecoin undertook a fast and said he would stick to it until the very last objector was freed. Civic Action groups went along with anarchists in leading processions, signing petitions, and visits to ministries.

At the end of twenty-one days, appeased by the promises of the government and convinced by his friends, the dear old man consented not to die. His fast struck a decisive blow in the fight to obtain a statute for conscientious objectors in France, and, as an after-effect, in Belgium.

The campaign of Nonviolent Civic Action in France was followed by no movement on a national scale. But groups and minigroups for research and action multiplied, and popularity of the idea grew, arousing enthusiasm in some and exasperation in others (the extreme right and the extreme left being equally exasperated).

IN FRANCE

Two pilots of the French military air force who had been posted to the nuclear tests in the Pacific, unable to ignore the criminal nature of their task, handed in their resignations, underwent the punishment this entailed, and, on their return, founded a center for meeting and coordination in Toulouse, called the 103.

Pastor René Cruze stood for election as President of the Republic. The long and the short of his program was the abolition of the Bomb. He has never hesitated to go out into the street followed by a line of his supporters holding on to the same chain as a symbol of our state of citizenship.

The Bishop of Orleans was a witness in the law court of that city and stood bail for two priests and a young teacher accused of sending back their draft cards. The latter, Jean-Marie Muller, has since won fame as the author of an excellent book entitled *The Gospel of Nonviolence,* and recently one entitled *The Tragedy of Nonviolence*, as well as by his lectures and fasts protesting the sale of firearms.

Jean Goss, although French—and more than French, Parisian —operates in other countries. His vigorous, popular, and prophetic speech is poured out to the prelates of the Vatican as well as to the crowds massed in the Red Square in Moscow. At the moment, aided by his wife, he is preaching nonviolence to the peoples of Latin America, converting trade-unionists, priests in training, and bishops. In Brazil, he succeeded in preventing bloodshed by bringing revolutionaries around to using the weapon of persuasion and proving its efficiency for themselves.

THE CROSS, THE FISH, AND THE CROZIER

In Recife in Brazil, fishermen ruined by a factory which was poisoning the coast with its waste, attempted to demonstrate, but the police barred their way. They sought the advice of their kind archbishop, who said to them, "Yes, demonstrations are forbidden, but not processions. I shall lead the procession and all you have to do is to follow me."

The cross advanced through the streets, veiled by a fishing net in which a dead fish swung to and fro. The archbishop, wearing his mitre, talked to the directors, the workmen, and the police as if to his children. "How many men do you need to dig filter ditches?"

"At least two thousand," was the answer.

"How many unemployed have we?"

"Ten thousand . . ."

Work began next day, and the fishermen returned to their nets.

We made the acquaintance of Dom Helder Camara of the wooden cross, Archbishop of Recife, in Rome during the Council. He received us with open arms. His arms open easily, like his heart. He promised to uphold our plea in the commissions charged with preparing the propositions put up to vote.

Seven of our Spanish friends, two of them girls, are in prison or on bail for having asked to be interned as a gesture of solidarity with José-Luis Beunza, a Catholic conscientious objector. Accompanied by volunteers of several countries, they set out from Geneva on foot, crossed France, and gave themselves up at the frontier in the Pyrenees.

So we are on the way to a Spanish statute of conscientious objectors.

CÉSAR CHAVEZ, CAPTAIN OF THE UNARMED[1]

It is not generally known throughout the world that in this second half of the twentieth century, in one of the most famed and prosperous sections in the United States, California, there can be found all the wretchedness of the poorest countries in the world. It is an agricultural country, but one of big-business farming, rich domains of thousands of acres, leveled, squared off, lined up, and exploited to the utmost.

All the former inhabitants of this earthly paradise—with its forests and birds, its winding rivers, its villages with their steeples, its fields and copses, its population of Spanish-speaking, Christianized Mexicans—were ruthlessly uprooted, driven out, and kept away.

The mass of farmworkers, whether native or imported from Puerto Rico or Japan, are hired for fruit picking and other jobs at the lowest wages and in the hardest conditions, and are then sent back to the dust they came from.

They work under the molten lead and quicklime of the sun dripping with sweat and grape juice, tormented by insects, poisoned by pesticides, with no drinking water near.

Social and medical assistance, a minimum living wage, time off, education for their children, contracts, the right to legal pro-

---

[1] No attempt has been made to update this section, written before 1970.—ed.

tection, pensions, all the benefits of the working class in other
states, are nonexistent here. Their status is much worse than
that of blacks.

Although there have been revolts, they were soon put down,
armed force being at the service of the big landowners. Strikes
are equally unavailing, since on the other side of the nearby
frontier, there are hordes of poor Mexicans waiting to replace
the unwilling.

César Chavez knew all this when, in 1962, he made up his
mind to form a trade union and harness the strength of the poor,
which is their number and their solidarity. He knew because he
was one of them, having been brought up in whatever camps his
parents chanced to find work. He differs from other workers
neither in stature nor in feature, but in genius and the virtues
that go to make a leader—and a nonviolent leader at that. They
are revealed whenever he talks to people, man to man, or to a
crowd.

He is poor and means to stay poor. He makes do with the
wage of the lowest of the low. Sparing with words, level-
headed, religious, he is firm, dignified, and respectful in his
relations with the adversary. For him, "human life is an absolute" which one must not attack at any cost.

He settled in Delano, the center of a vine-growing valley,
and worked quietly for three years grouping, organizing, and
educating his campaigners.

Then he launched them into a strike and upheld them in it
for five years. By marching to Sacramento, he drew the attention
of the whole country to his movement and to the justice of his
cause, for which he gained the support of the workers' trade
unions, the liberals, and the Church.

The fight on the spot was hard. Pickets were subjected to endless harassment. They could no longer simply be shot as before,
or tarred and feathered as people had been in 1933. But they

could be sprayed with sulfate, smothered in dust, or "accidentally" injured by maneuvering tractors.

Besides, it was very difficult to prevent strikebreakers, brought in surreptitiously, from acting. The workers were needy, and driven to desperation, and if they had to give up grapepicking, how were they to live? Fatigue and despair, and worse still, anger, were getting the better of them.

So Chavez, after a twenty-five-day fast, broadened the maneuver and dispersed his men throughout the territory, posting his pickets in front of supermarkets and big shops in town and going up and down the country himself, calling the public to his aid. His appeal was heard as far away as Canada, and even in England. The sale of grapes decreased, boxes of them were thrown into the sea, dockers refused to load them into ships.

The potentates capitulated one after the other.

The struggle is still going on and has spread to other regions.

It is not a question of wages, but of dignity. "A revolution of heart and mind." It is not a question of politics or ideology. It is a question of health, education, conscience, and human relations between men.

CONVERSION WITHIN THE CHURCH

The immense progress the Catholic Church has made along the path of peace with Pope John XXIII's *"Pacem in Terris"* and since then, cannot be ignored. In the first place, on its own ground of religious reconciliation, it has made overtures to the Oriental and the Anglican high churches, and has put an end to the interdicts and curses it once laid on Freemasons and Communists.

Its interventions on behalf of social justice (peace between the nations and respect of all men, whatever their race, creed, or culture) have become more and more insistent and precise.

In addition to Dom Helder Camara, several bishops in Latin America have taken up the cause of the poor, and some of them have shared our church land.

The Assembly of the Bishops of France rose up against torture during the Algerian war. At Oran, in the thick of the gunfire from all sides, a priest came out of the church, his arms wide open, and crossed the square. The guns fell silent.

The word "nonviolence" has not yet made its appearance in the encyclical. It has crept into the "Pastoral Constitution" of the Council in the shape of *"sine violentia."* It becomes explicit, and more and more so, in the proclamations of Paul VI.

A few hot-headed monks and worker priests, ready to give up the chalice in favor of the machine gun, have indeed tried to preach the "theology of violence," which is nothing more than the warmed-over remains of "just war." But Mother Church has no intention of ratifying this error.

Cardinal Ottaviani, in his study of traditional doctrine, notes that not one of the reasons brought forward by St. Thomas in justification of war can be applied to modern war. And this is certainly not a justification of civil war.

Finally, the Vatican commissions, beginning with those of North America, have boldly taken up all the arguments discreetly put forward by the Council and, mindful of the virile virtues of evangelical nonviolence, have given back to salt its salty savor.

THE TWO GREAT DISCOVERIES
OF THE CENTURY

There is an answer and a compensation to the two world wars of the twentieth century. That answer, that compensation, is the Gandhian Saga.

Let him hear who hath ears to hear! Let whoever is not deafened by fear and noise, nor blinded by lucre and hate, grasp the meaning of this parallel! And let no one say that Providence is not on the watch or that the world is absurd!

The two great discoveries of our century are the atomic bomb, and the force of truth or nonviolence! It is not by chance that they have been revealed at the same time. There is a logical link between them: that of the Power of Darkness with Light, that of Life with Death. And now logic requires us to choose!

Whoever does not resolutely choose the narrow path of nonviolence and go upstream against the common current works along with the others at making the Bomb and manufacturing his own death. The Bomb is the supreme masterpiece of modern science and technique. It is the goal and the end of every enterprise of this civilization. It is the system's signature. Let whoever hath eyes read and spell out the signature: S A T A N.

THE FUTURE

What is the future of nonviolence in the West? The question might just as easily be put in these terms: Has the West a future?

For it is obvious that national and social rivalry on the one hand, and the excrescence of science and technology on the other, lead, like two rails, straight to the abyss.

The good news, the only eternally good thing, is that another road is open.

We must not discard it as being too easy: the road to peace is not restful! The road is rough that leads the meek to their inheritance of the earth!

Neither must we turn away from it because we believe it to be impossible, nor say with disastrous modesty, "We are not saints."

It is a question of being men, of not perishing body and soul.

APPENDIX I

An article from L'Express *on Lanza del Vasto's fast*

NONVIOLENCE
Twenty-Day Fast

In this quarter of Clichy where the houses are so squat and black that they remind one of miners' cottages in the north of France, there has been an unusual stir as Holy Week begins. Young people, reporters, priests in cassocks, and pastors in plain clothes go in and out of a little door in the rue du Landy. Three very thin men, bearded and dressed in brown trousers and sky-blue smocks, with esparto and canvas shoes on their bare feet, stroll about in a covered courtyard furnished with classroom benches. They are Bernard Gaschard, a farmer, Pierre Parodi, a doctor, and Lanza del Vasto, a writer.

All three began a public, twenty-day fast on the thirty-first of March. Until the eve of Easter Sunday, they will take nothing but water. None of them has ever fasted more than ten days. One of Lanza del Vasto's companions is very weak. The reason for their voluntary ordeal is the Algerian war and the atrocities perpetrated by both sides.

Two Tragedies

Several events have driven these disciples of nonviolence to this extreme gesture. A friend from the community they have founded in Bollène (Vaucluse) was murdered a year ago in a Tunisian *suk*. His fellow soldiers called him "Christ." He had refused to carry arms and spent his time caring for the sick and disabled. Several hundred Moslems thronged to his funeral.

One of the "Companions" of the "Ark" (the name of their community) recently returned from Algeria where he witnessed the torture inflicted on a Moslem suspect aged twenty-six, a boxer named Mouloud Medaouri. After twenty-four hours of cruel treatment, the young Algerian died.

These atrocities, committed by both sides, have made Lanza del Vasto come out of the semiretirement into which he withdrew after the Liberation.

The writer, a tall man with penetrating blue eyes, was converted to nonviolence in the course of a two-year journey through India in 1936, when he discovered swamis, gurus, and Gandhi, a strange universe of mystery, the absolute and holiness, described in his famous *Return to the Source*.

The personality of Gandhi and the concrete results of "Bapu's" nonviolent action deeply impressed him. On his way back from the East, mostly on foot, he made his plans to create an "ashram" (a Gandhian community) in France. But when he reached Jerusalem, the sight of tanks patroling in front of sacred places met his eyes, and in 1938, the alarm bell of Czechoslovakia tolled for the death of all hope of peace in the West. During the war, he meditated, worked, wrote, and cast the foundations of a new order, the Ark, open to all believers.

An Overwhelming Appeal

In 1945 and 1946, many young people used to go and listen to his "Commentary on the Gospels" given in an old house in the St. Paul Quarter in Paris. With a few of them, he founded his first community at Tournier. The life led there was like that in a Hindu ashram: manual work, total poverty, a vegetarian diet, a refusal of the machinery and technical instruments of modern life. Yoga exercises help the disciples toward meditation and spiritual life. Thirty-five people, including women and children, now live at Bollène to which the community moved two years ago.[1] The order consists of only a score of Companions, who have taken vows. But its influence is infinitely out of proportion to this small number.

Many religious were deeply moved by the "Appeal to the Conscience of the French Nation" and the "Appeal to Leaders of the National Liberation Front" which Lanza launched at the beginning of his fast. Several Parisian vicars invited him to come and spend the rest of his fast in their parishes. All over the country, in the capital and in the provinces, believers of every denomination, reservists, and students joined the fast. In Strasburg, Catholic, Protestant, and Jewish students observed a fast day at the beginning of Ramadan. In Algeria itself, many Moslems, who disapprove of the crimes perpetrated by both sides, were profoundly moved by the unprecedented gesture. In Morocco, the weekly newspaper *Al Istiqlal* published the complete text of the author's appeal for nonviolence.

April 19, 1957

---

[1] The Community moved to La Borie Noble in Hérault in 1966.

APPENDIX II

An article from Le Canard Enchaîné[1]
on the eve of the Carpentras trial

FOUR CRIMINALS

Today, Wednesday November 22, 1961, the trial opens, at Carpentras, of four dangerous individuals, namely Joseph Pyronnet, Marie Faugeron, Simone Pacot, and Jacques Tinel, the leading members of "Nonviolent Civic Action" accused of "inciting soldiers to disobedience." Always ahead of other newspapers, the *Canard* has been able to get a copy of the accusation which will be read by the public prosecutor. Here is the document:

Gentlemen of the Jury, you see here before you four public evil-doers of the most fearsome species, the nonviolent species. To put it plainly, four advocates of non-murder!

At the moment we are living (if I dare say so, for it is the moment so many others are dying), the action of these criminals is a veritable challenge to our institutions and to society. Indeed, gentlemen, if by misfortune their doctrine were to triumph, the whole foundation of French life would be shaken. The government set up by the violence of the thirtieth of May would collapse as if from a bazooka kick

---

[1] A humorous, satirical newspaper. Literally, "The Chained Duck." *Canard* is also slang for "newspaper."

in the heart. Our compatriots would no longer experience the virile suspense of wondering whether, when they get home, they will find their flats destroyed by unknown plastic-bombers who do not share their public opinions, or even whether some stray bullet or a dagger stuck into the nape of their neck will not hinder them from getting home.

I shall stop there, gentlemen. The case has been stated.

I beg you, gentlemen, to inflict the heaviest penalty on these contemptible creatures. In consequence of which, I trust that you will request the Keeper of the Seals to refuse these criminals the benefit of the political regime in prison, for they might contaminate the heroes of one or other of the parties. Let us never forget that nonviolent fallout is even more dangerous than that of the atomic bomb.

Thanks to you, gentlemen of the jury at Carpentras, thanks to your historic verdict, nonviolence shall not pass!

R. Treno

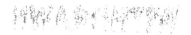

A NOTE ON THE TYPE

The text of this book was set on the Linotype in Garamond No. 3, a modern rendering of the type first cut by Claude Garamond (1510-1561). Garamond was a pupil of Geoffrey Troy and is believed to have based his letters on the Venetian models, although he introduced a number of important differences, and it is to him we owe the letter which we know as old-style. He gave to his letters a certain elegance and a feeling of movement that won for their creator an immediate reputation and the patronage of Francis I of France.

Composed by The Haddon Craftsmen, Inc.,
Scranton, Pa. Printed and bound by
The Colonial Press, Inc., Clinton, Mass.
Typography and binding design by Virginia Tan.